WRITING
YOUR WAY

D1500984

Darling, these are the most difficult words I've ever had to say:
paleoanthropic, hypochondriasis, deuteranopia,
sesquicentennial, anthropomorphism....

WRITING YOUR WAY

Peter Stillman

BOYNTON/COOK PUBLISHERS, INC.
UPPER MONTCLAIR, NEW JERSEY 07043

Library of Congress Cataloging in Publication Data

Stillman, Peter.
   Writing your way.

   Summary: A textbook designed to help students develop
individual writing skills suitable for a variety of purposes.
    1. English language—Composition and exercises.
[1. English language—Composition and exercises] I. Title.
PE1408.S764 1983   808'.042   83-15820
ISBN 0-86709-067-7

©1984 by Boynton/Cook Publishers Inc.
All rights reserved. No part of this book may be used or reproduced in any
manner without written permission except in the case of brief quotations
embodied in critical articles and reviews.

For information address Boynton/Cook Publishers, Inc.
P.O. Box 860, Upper Montclair, New Jersey 07043

Printed in the United States of America
       86 87 88 10 9 8 7 6 5 4 3

Acknowledgments

AMY DOCKSER. "Chronicle," reprinted by permission of the author. The article appeared in both *Writer's Digest* (12/80) and *Young People Today*.

NEW DIRECTIONS PUBLISHING CORPORATION. "The Red Wheelbarrow" from *Collected Earlier Poems of William Carlos Williams*. Copyright 1938 by New Directions. "A Sort of Song" from *Collected Later Poems of William Carlos Williams*. Copyright 1944, 1948 by William Carlos Williams. Both reprinted by permission of the publisher.

THE NEW YORK TIMES. "A New Dig Unearths the Pathos of Vesuvius" by Philip M. Boffey, November 17, 1982; "Prudent Spiders Weave Keep-off-the-web Sign" by Bayard Webster, January 9, 1983. © 1982/83 by The New York Times Company. Reprinted by permission.

SCOTT, FORESMAN AND COMPANY. Interview with Andy Rooney from English Highlights, Spring 1982. Copyright © 1982 by Scott, Foresman and Company. Reprinted by permission of the publisher and Mr. Rooney.

HELEN THURBER. "The Bear Who Let It Alone" from *Fables for Our Time* by James Thurber, published by Harper & Row. Copyright © 1940 by James Thurber. Copyright © 1968 by Helen Thurber. From *Selected Letters of James Thurber*, eds. Helen Thurber and Edwards Weeks (1980), the letter appearing on page 198 addressed to Messrs. Kussow and Chopin. Both reprinted by permission of Helen Thurber.

Foreword to the Teacher

In a teacher's guide I wrote to accompany this text I went on for about thirty pages about why much of what we teach in the name of writing instruction may be dangerous to the nation's health; how traditional, best-selling composition texts are a mix of hokum, hoax and hot air; why we've been forced to teach to socio-curricular imperatives that we know don't apply in the real world; where writing comes from, what it's for, and why it's vital; and how and why this book will nudge young people into knowing that they're writers—not just able to write, but *writers*—and that knowing it is like discovering ice cream.

As a teacher's guide it's...well, somewhat unorthodox. Nowhere in it is there a set of marching orders, a spelled-out means of how to get from Monday to Friday, or a scripted answer to the question fired at you from the third row, last seat: "I read all this stuff. Now what am I supposed to do?" The guide is a bit unorthodox because the book is too, and early in the writing of it I had to face the fact that people looking for a conventional lock-step approach to composing—a program wherein everyone with stamina and grit will arrive on the same square on the same day—are going to buy another book or, worse, a series of them.

Writing isn't a linear process; what happens on a Wednesday doesn't depend on what was covered Monday. What materializes on Susan's paper will not—should not—be remotely like what appears on Fred's. And what is so quirky, so elusively lovely, so exciting about writing isn't discoverable through step-by-step exercises, class-wide assignments on such electrifying topics as "My Favorite Surprise," or drills on the expository paragraph (whatever that is). So I didn't put any of that stuff in this book. I did try to make it honest and readable, even amusing for stretches, which is no small thing.

I wish you'd read the teacher's guide, which is, more accurately, a rationale based on the proposition that students aren't created equal, an explication and condensation of modern theory about the writing process, and finally, a set of suggestions about how this book can work for you and your students. If you don't have the guide, however, or the time to read it, let me explain briefly what this book is about—what it hopes to accomplish (and actually *has,* in a number of classroom situations), and why it's important that you and not just your students write your way through it.

Taped to the wall over my desk are two statements about the teaching of writing. The first was issued by a best-selling writer, lecturer and TV celebrity. It goes, "The trouble with teaching young people to write is that they don't have anything to say yet, so you have to fall back on teaching them form." The second observation is by Nancy Martin, an eminent teacher and writer about writing: "Young people need their own topics as well as their own language.... Teachers suppose that students cannot write without suggested topics and marks—and, indeed, unless the context is changed, they cannot."

These sentiments—and you've heard them again and again—represent two totally different points of view. I offer them here because, like it or not, they are also valid tests of what we really believe about writing and writers—what we personally hold to be true, beyond the dictates of curriculum, beyond the ponderous authority of textbooks, beyond the exhortations of college instructors. If you subscribe generally to statement A, you number in the majority of teachers committed to dealing mainly with *form* and the myriad rhetorical and mechanical conventions that attach to that commitment. If, however, you find yourself on the side of statement B, you're in the company of a growing body of teachers who believe that "the context" does need changing—that given the chance young people *do* have something of their own to say on paper and ample linguistic depth to say it with conviction and power. You're persuaded that dwelling week after week, year after year, on mechanical correctness, on puerile essay topics, on grammar-as-the-road-to-competency amounts to a protracted game with more losers than winners.

You're also stuck for good teaching material and maybe too for a sound rebuttal to the charge that letting young people sit there and just write, for Heaven's sake, isn't teaching them *anything*. I've tried herein to provide the former, which, along with your own insights and enthusiasm, will generate the latter: good writing, students eager to put themselves on paper, not only in English class but elsewhere too.

Most composition texts I've examined are, despite their surface differences, much the same: what writing is ultimately *for*, they agree with iron fixity, is (a) producing expository essays for college, and (b) conducting business. Writing's goals have long been in the service of such "preparations for life"; ironically, they haven't addressed the broader matter of life itself—of how writing can and should be a life-long engagement for all of us, not just the few who have a "knack" for it. Because we cannot possibly determine how and in what forms writing should work in anyone's life, it's both pedagogically wise and humane to offer young people opportunities to discover that writing is as liberal and liberating as speech itself—that it isn't primarily utilitarian; that in various ways it's a vital and sustaining part of human behavior. Together you and I can push them to this awareness by inviting them to write without fear of censure, to write about the stuff of their particular worlds, to arrive at the realization that writing isn't a print-out of learning, but *is* learning, meaning-making of a kind that will serve them long past college.

These chapters are meant to be ways for young people to discover. For this reason they don't conclude with exercises or "My Favorite Surprise" essay topics. You can't ask someone to be entirely herself on paper and then after explaining why and how, hit her with an assignment that demands the opposite. Students see through such phoniness and rightly so. The book's tone may bother you at first; you may sense that the teacher has been written out of it. That's not really the case: these chapters are rough ways only, meant to be adapted, improvised on, even occasionally ignored. You're the maestro, not I. Furthermore, I mean deeply what the book's title suggests: it *is* about writing *your* way, and that being the case, it made sense to address the book's real audience in real language and not in the condescending prose that textbooks generally use.

About your writing along with your students: I think it's nearly impossible to write in the ways I've suggested in here without coming to some powerful revelations of your own about what writing is and what its importances are. That at least is what happened to me. Moreover, it's generally acknowledged to be a good idea to let students see you writing too and thus to begin sensing that writing *is* a real-world form of behavior and not just another misery visited on youth by adult authority figures. It shouldn't amount to extra work. Your paper-correcting load will reduce drastically and much more class time will be spent writing. (A decided bonus is that when you do read a batch of student papers, you'll probably enjoy the experience.)

This is a different kind of writing text, but not a visionary one. It asks young writers to go off in their own directions; it urges them to get up at dawn and fill pages; it promotes talking about writing, sharing it with peers, reading out loud, recording family folklore, cartooning, letter-writing, journal-keeping, and sometimes being downright silly on paper; it pushes them to get so hooked on writing that they'll feel guilty about taking a day off. It urges them, in other words, to do what writers do. That young people *are* writers isn't a naively hopeful assertion. I've seen the truth of it too often to write a book based on any less substantial thesis.

Not that this is one man's elaborately worked-out point of view. According to NEA's *Today's Education*, "The best programs for sharpening classroom skills are those that understand that the more writing teachers discover about themselves as writers, the better able they are to work with their student writers. No program understands that point better than the Bread Loaf School of English...in Vermont." To which I add a hearty *Amen*. Dixie Goswami, the Writing Program's director and herself a uniquely gifted teacher of teachers, annually draws to Bread Loaf a group of experts on the writing process—such eminent figures as Ann Berthoff, Jimmy Britton, Peter Elbow, Janet Emig, Shirley Brice Heath, Ken Macrorie, and Nancy Martin, for example. Bread Loaf's faculty and students together form the most intellectually stimulating community I've ever lived in. This book came out of two summers there (and most specifically out of a penciled note on one of my papers: "Peter, you've simply got to write a book. Dixie"). If you're a reader about writing, you'll be quick to recognize the imprint of two people whose ideas and practices have profoundly influenced me—Ann Berthoff and Ken Macrorie.

Most publishers wouldn't have touched this project with a barge-pole. But Bob Boynton did, and not because he's an old friend. Boynton/Cook's rapid rise to eminence among teachers who care about writing is a direct result of Bob's caring about it. I'm grateful—both for the friendship and the sharp editing. Thanks too to Sandy Boynton, who doesn't earn her living as an editor but who pinned my ears back for some early, hopelessly fuzzy passages—and who had better things to do with her talent than take time out to design a cover and some delightful illustrations.

Finally, thanks to Ann Stillman, my wife, tireless manuscript reader, critic and prop. For better or worse, this book simply wouldn't have happened without her.

Contents

Dedication

for Bill Cook

1

Writing Your Way

By producing the kind of writing their teachers seem to want, students hope to gain a good mark. Over the years they lose the six-year-old's sense of having something to say of their own.

Nancy Martin

This book is meant to help you write *your* way, not somebody else's. For one thing, it isn't stuffed with rules and exercises. For another, it doesn't offer you any long-range, step-by-step procedures that assume your ignorance when you begin and your mastery when you finish. There's no proof anywhere that good writing comes out of any such procedure—that you and I must start on the same square to get to the same destination. In fact, writing may not be learnable in any systematic way, or if it is, no one has discovered that way.

Writing isn't just a device to prove that you do (or don't) do your homework; that you have absorbed so much information; that you're capable of writing an essay without misspellings or wrong punctuation; that you "know how to write" as well as you should for your age and grade. Your words on paper can provide any or all of these proofs and still be empty and mechanical. You can write "correctly" without saying anything much, and you can get "better" at it from year to year just by making fewer mistakes and by playing it safe. Throughout the long process of your education you can earn passing grades in writing without ever realizing that you're a writer and have been all along; and you can become so bound up by complicated rules that the real writer in you is silenced.

Writing is not meant primarily to be a means to measure you against rules and class standards. Its deeper and far more exciting function is to serve as a way to find shapes and names for the world as *you* have come to know it; to make meaning; to find on paper what you know and feel. It's an extremely important way for you to test your understandings against another's, your reader's; to capture what seems important or lovely or puzzling before it passes; to know the joy and pride that come when a line appears on paper that matches closely a thought in your head, especially when a reader is pleased too.

None of these ways has anything to do with writing for a grade or doing exercises; they have to do with rediscovering what you probably sensed when you were six or seven—that *writing is a way of learning and knowing*. When we get used to writing mostly as a device for proving that we can avoid errors or as a way to print out what we're required to know, much of what writing should be in our lives is missed. This isn't an argument against homework, essays, or tests or any other kind of writing that measures your achievements as a student. If, however, your understanding of writing has narrowed only to this, what follows should be very useful, even exciting, not only now but for the rest of your life.

This book urges you to fill blank paper with the stuff of your world and no one else's. This may be bothersome at first, for you may be unused to such invitations. It asks that you take some risks on paper—that you write in ways and about matters that may not result in what you recognize as a "good" paper, something to be passed in to earn a grade. This book doesn't have models to follow, except that you'll find yourself learning more about possible forms for your writing as you read the many pieces of good writing in these chapters.

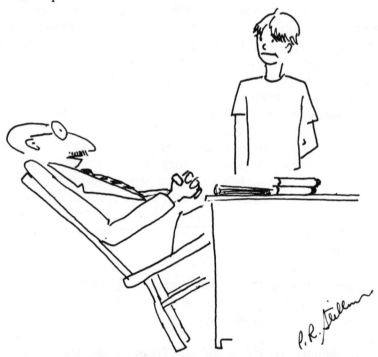

*Perhaps I'm being unfair, Robert, but when a student paper begins with
"Fourscore and seven years ago," I get suspicious.*

This isn't a "skills"-centered book. Spelling, punctuation, and capitalization are necessary parts of writing, but they don't *amount to* writing. Eventually, some of your work will reach a more or less finished form. Near this point, you'll want to be sure that such mechanical matters are dealt with—

that the piece is up to the standards you would expect to find in any writing meant for public reading. But writers of any age who let these matters worry them at an early stage run the risk of having what they want to say swept away by the dread of incorrect spelling or punctuating. If somewhere near the finish of a piece you remain confused about parts of its mechanics, you can and should seek out someone with an eye for spotting errors. You can also consult a handbook. *Wanting* to get their better writings into finished public shape is what finally forces writers to learn more about mechanical skills. Reading helps too. Writers are readers.

*   *   *

What does this book ask of you? Many things, the first of which is that you hold off saying either "I can't," "I won't," or "Writing stinks (or bores me) and that's that." Furthermore, you're asked not to be chiefly interested in writing for a grade. This doesn't amount to asking you to fail English or any other subject that requires writing, nor on the other hand your taking a free ride—scribbling away with no thought to how others will respond to what you put on paper. Some writing is private, not meant for others' judgment. But much writing *is* eventually meant to be judged, if only informally by an interested reader. Grading is only one form of judgment—a narrow and not always useful one. You can "pass"—earn a 75 or 80—by turning in some pretty awful stuff, as you know. But when you write to say something that's important to you, that you think is worth someone else's reading, you're not going to want the kind of judgment that can be boiled down to a number or a letter. You're going to itch to know whether you've hit or missed. It will make you a tougher, wiser judge of your own writing too. You may not always feel up to the effort of working on a piece that will hit, but when you do, you won't stop when you figure you've given seventy-five percent of yourself. You'll be more demanding than the toughest teacher you've ever had.

You're going to be pushed to write much more than you probably do now. If you don't write at least four or five times a week, it'll be like starting from scratch whenever you do. I'm not talking about homework; I'm talking about *writing*, and they're frequently not the same. The only way to find out about yourself as a writer is to write. Sooner or later, if you keep at it honestly and faithfully, the joy in it will surface. Even now you're closer to this point than you probably realize. You're not just a raw beginner. Much of the necessary instruction, the basics, lies behind you. If you think of yourself only as a *student* writer, you'll probably continue to think of writing as some kind of practice for the real thing in the future. In this book you're urged to write, never to practice-write.

In a way, classrooms are perfect settings for writers. Although writing itself is mostly a solitary pursuit, you daily find yourself surrounded by others who may be equally interested in finding out more about themselves as writers. Most adults are forced to work alone and to try their final writings out on strangers. For what's in this book to be useful to you, plan on working in small groups (and occasionally larger ones). This way you'll be able to get and give feedback, reader reaction and advice. You'll have an audience made up of acquaintances, not distant strangers. You may find this awkward and uncomfortable at first, but if you're serious, it'll work for you. Enough of this kind of experience and your writing will sharpen; you'll be trying to reach others rather than simply writing in a vacuum with no live readers in mind. A byproduct of this experience—and also something older writers miss—is that you'll talk more about writing too, and while talk isn't the same as writing, it's a highly useful way to find out how you and others understand it and deal with its problems.

HOW TO FILE YOUR WRITING

Right   Wrong

If you don't keep a writing folder, you should. Writers, young ones especially, throw words into wastebaskets rather than saving them. If you do, it's probably proof that you attach no importance to yourself on paper or may even dislike yourself there. While you can't be blamed for dumping a quiz paper or an essay you cranked out in fifteen minutes strictly because you needed something to hand in, beware the wastebasket habit. Approach writing the way you're asked to in here and you could end up tossing out important pieces of yourself. You can't tell whether an honest attempt on paper is a failure until you've let it cool off for awhile. Trashing it too soon could be a sorry mistake. Except for the most obviously useless stuff, put what you write in a folder (which isn't, by the way, a portable wastebasket; devise a system that'll allow you to retrieve material without dumping the contents on the floor).

When you feel a need to disagree with parts of this book, do so. You may find it occasionally silly or confusing or for stretches uninteresting. It's not reasonable to expect that every page of any book is going to work for you. Modify whenever you think you should—reshape my suggestions to fit you as a writer. But believe—take the book to heart. Much of what's in here is put as lightly as I knew how, but that doesn't mean that the book's purpose is mainly to amuse. I'll be delighted if you enjoy the reading more than you typically do when you open a textbook. Don't be misled, however.

What's being asked of you is, if you respond honestly to it, as tough as anything you've ever tackled, in or out of school. You've got to respond to what is asked in here, which means sticking at it—writing just about every day, and not the kind of going-through-the-motions junk that you and I and every writer over ten can turn out with his brain shut off. I think you'll have fun doing it much of the time, but fun isn't the object.

*   *   *

There's little need to explain how this book is arranged. In fact, it very nearly isn't; any chapter in here could be nearly anyplace else; or all of them should be first. When you're writing, everything's going on at once; it's a complete act, not parts of one. You may find some chapters easier to deal with than others, but nowhere should you have to read one chapter to get through another. In other words, you needn't "master" anything in order to "master" something else. When you're done, you won't be master of anything other than the demon that sends you running from writing.

Are some experiences in here more important than others? Probably, but this can't really be determined until you've tried them, so try them, all of them. That's how the book is meant to be used. Furthermore, you're expected to keep going back, retrying earlier experiences. When you do—and do it often—you'll find that they'll keep changing for you. *Writers should never abandon early experiences that worked.* Good writing isn't a distant destination that requires you to leave behind what's familiar. This should help explain why the book is more circular than straight. Throughout you'll find yourself using with more depth of understanding the same things you've dealt with before.

There's much writing in here from younger writers and some from older ones, mainly me. None of it represents the "right way," because in writing there probably isn't any right way; there are only ways that work and ways that don't work. I can't tell you which ways will work for you, but I can assure you that you'll find the ways, and not just because I say so.

Some of what's in here may strike you as being purely play—fun and games with pen or pencil. Most of this kind of writing invitation is short and pops up in unexpected places. Writing is a serious business, but it's also a medium meant for amusement—of oneself or others. When you're offered an invitation for having fun on paper, accept it; there's a real danger in taking *any* subject too seriously. Meanwhile, though, you'll be put to some stiffer stuff and also introduced to some practices that at first may not be pure pleasure—keeping up a journal, for example; making a near-daily practice of going off by yourself to jot down whatever comes; dashing down notes in a pocket scribbler; disciplining yourself to read your writing aloud; using certain writing techniques as a way to understand other school subjects, as well as the world you live in. In short, writing, writing, writing.

2

"Of Myself, for Myself"

I imagine that the notebook is about other people. But of course it is not.

Joan Didion

(9/8/81)

Hiked up the trail at dawn today to pick the last of the blackberries for breakfast. A fawn stood suddenly in the track. We looked at each other for a moment; then she vanished. Poof. Gone. I love the way deer disappear.

· · ·

Heard last night about someone with a tumor as big as a grapefruit. Ella N. told about it—some cousin in Ohio. Always tumors are described as being grapefruit-size. Wouldn't it be odd to hear about a grapefruit the size of a tumor?

· · ·

Three crows are sitting in my poplar tree. I have the uncomfortable feeling they're talking about me.

(10/1/81)

Raining. Shining roads. Pimpling puddles. Mud. Mud. Mud. Rain-shining, puddle-pimpled, muddy roads; splash-bang potholes; star-soaking, moon-bruising rain. We-sure-need-the-rain kind of rain.

· · ·

A "shunpike," I heard on the radio last night, is an area term for someone who avoids straight highways (pikes) in favor of winding lanes. What a fine little word.

· · ·

Would love to see again *The Mummy's Curse*, the movie that scared me silly when I was a kid. Mummy walked with locked knees, right arm sticking out stiff as a 4x4. Killed most of the people in the movie with it but couldn't move more than maybe a half-mile an hour. Was it Lon Chaney who played the part? Impossible to recognize under all that bandaging. Ancient Egyptians must have emptied whole drugstores wrapping up a mummy. Here he comes, shuffling out of his tomb, arm out like the gate on a tollbooth. Glog!

Another dead archaeologist, never a gurgle. Little kids hiding under movie seats screaming, popcorn boxes flying all over the place: "Lemme know when he's gone, Louie!"

(3/20/82)

Saw printed on a waiter's t-shirt: " 'Now that we've seen each other,' said the unicorn, 'I'll believe in you if you believe in me.'

Lewis Carroll"

(easy scene to imagine: ...The little girl looked at the unicorn without alarm but with considerable interest. Its eyes, she noted, were blue. The way the sun touched them made it look as if tiny golden clouds floated across them.

The unicorn was chewing, slowly and with much dignity, its lower jaw slurring from side to side in the manner that some very old people chew. It continued to look down at the little girl, who had grass-brown hair. "Good afternoon," it said.

"You talked with your mouth full," she answered.)

Can you think of any reasons why the writer of this stuff bothered to put it on paper? It doesn't resemble the kind of writing we can classify as essay or report, poem or news article. It jumps around, offering the reader only a string of unconnected bits that might or might not be pieces of something else. It almost seems, doesn't it, that these odd little whatever-they-are's were never meant to be printed in a book for others to read? That the writing is so wrapped up in the writer and so unfinished that our reading almost amounts to snooping?

...then after I took his gun away, I threw him and his partner up against the wall and said....

These are, of course, journal entries, mine; they're being used here partly as proof that journals aren't necessarily meant to be read by others, and also to persuade you that a journal can and probably should include anything at all that seems likely *to you* at the moment. Maybe, too, these sample entries will demonstrate that (a) even if, as I've heard a hundred young writers say, "Nothing happened today," you can still find something worth jotting in your journal; and (b) a journal comes as close as any writing can to reflecting the private and often wacky ways our minds dart and meander just under the smooth surface we let the rest of the world see. Also (and very importantly), a journal is the perfect place to store what may eventually turn into more public forms of writing. The deer in the path, for example, became this:

> An owl lives in the hemlock tree.
> Last year it did the same.
> Still heaven-hung's the mousing hawk,
> Its shadow grown quite tame.
>
> Fall waits like drying shutters propped
> Against a leaning sky,
> Scant challenge for the rhymer
> To catch and versify.
>
> Yet twenty crumpled pages past
> My berrying at dawn
> I've failed to trap in poetry
> A foolish, frightened fawn.

It shouldn't be difficult to see in these entries a half-dozen other possibilities that could find expression in any number of ways.

Journals are usually *chronological*—kept in order of time and dated—but they don't have to be records of the often-boring details of this day or that. A journal should, if fact, be a clear proof that being you isn't boring, even on those days when we shrug and say "Nothing happened." Too many journals I've looked at seem meant to establish just the opposite, beginning each entry with such exciting stuff as "Got up. Took a shower. Had breakfast. Caught the bus for school." Etc. Even a goldfish would have more interesting matters to note. The routine things in life—the experiences nearly everyone has from day to day—*are* boring and furthermore have nothing to do with the unique individual who lives inside the person going robot-like through the same morning routine as millions of others. The truth is that scarcely a moment goes by in your life that doesn't hold something worth jotting down; and although a journal needn't be a daily matter, no day is ever empty of material.

Henry David Thoreau, this country's most quoted journal-keeper, described his journals as being "of myself, for myself." What he meant, I think, is that a journal is a fine way to capture life as each of us sees, understands, and reacts to it. Better to do that than just to live life out, never noting the particulars that together make each of us who we are and very different from the rest. He also meant that a journal has for its audience the *self*—and this can be the most sensitive and important audience most of us will ever know.

"Of myself, for myself." There's a pleasant ring of privacy and freedom about those words. Nowhere in them is there a hint that a person's journal should satisfy any requirements beyond his own. Even if you're required to keep a journal—and I'm requesting it—your journal should remain *yours*; you shouldn't be keeping it to satisfy someone else. If a fragment floats to the surface and draws you into ten pages of frantic scribbling, fine; don't worry about spelling, organization, neatness; just get it down. Only one concern bouncing around in your head? That was sometimes a day's worth of journal-keeping for Thoreau, as well as for a student of mine who recorded on a particular day only this: "Today my stupid rabbit died." Nothing is too silly, painful, crazy-sounding, angry, sentimental, corny, trivial, or important to go into a journal—not if at the moment it is *of yourself* and *for yourself*. Just one rule applies: Don't write phony or puffed-up stuff. If you can't sound like you in your journal, where else can you?

(One ticklish point: Put terribly confidential stuff in a journal and you'll probably spend part of every day worried sick that someone will get hold of it. This isn't an empty fear; even the most trustworthy people have a touch of the snoop in them. I can recall a couple of upsetting, embarrassing situations growing out of parents' reading through journals and discovering things that shocked them. You must be the judge of what goes into your journal and what doesn't.)

So far this talk about journal-keeping has been kind of vague. By attempting to avoid telling you exactly what to put in a journal and how you should keep it, I've left you with mostly generalized comments. When students asked, "What am I supposed to keep in a journal?" it rarely helped when I told them, "Anything that seems to belong there," or "Whatever ideas and experiences seem worthwhile." This often led to pages of neatly dated entries that began, "Got out of bed. Took a shower, etc." Saying that a journal can include *anything* led students to space-fill with strings of *nothing*, and looking back, I can't blame them. Listing subjects to write about didn't work either. Such a list was originally planned for this unit but ended up in the wastebasket because it sounded like a bunch of composition topics, and that's exactly what a journal *isn't* for. What should be helpful and interesting is a list of possible journal *functions*:

- A journal can be a place for putting incidents and events that, although they're small, provide examples of larger concerns we believe to be important. Here's such an entry from the journal of Ralph Waldo Emerson, 19th century scholar and writer:

(1862)
I like people who can do things. When Edward and I struggled in vain to drag our big calf into the barn, the Irish girl put her finger into the calf's mouth, and led her in directly.

This is from a student's journal:

(2/1/80)

How I hate the cold. Hearing the morning ski report reminds me every day how much I dread winter. Harry Duffy on the radio makes being wet and freezing sound like fun, but his cheerful report only makes me feel colder.

- Think of your journal as being a net for catching shining particles from the day:

(4/12/81)

When I watch water pour forth from the lip of the pitcher pump in the kitchen, I'm as fascinated as Isaac Newton must have been when Nature whispered in his dozing ear, "This is how it works—this is how the whole thing works." Sometimes I stand there and pump just to watch the water come sparkling out.

(3/28/82)

I paused at my chores tonight when a flock of Canada geese flew over. I couldn't see them until they moved across the moon. Then they were gone again, trailing behind them their wild, anxious *cree-onk*-ing yodel.

- Historians use the journals of ordinary people like you and me to find out about the past. This doesn't mean that journal-keepers try to record *history*. It's enough that a journal be one person's view of how life is. Someday it will become a view of how it *was*. And that's what history is. Here are samples of two journals, both from an earlier time. Neither reads like a history book, but both let us discover parts of the past. The first records the events of one day in the Adirondack Mountains in 1851; the second covers three days in central Africa. It was written in 1827.

A.

(Tuesday 16th)

It is difficult to describe the sensation one feels in camping out for the first time. You lie down upon a bed of hemlock boughs which is soft & fragrant as a bed of roses—above the dark blue sky glittering with stars—at your feet a roasting fire, which blazes & crackles & throws up the merry sparks—the very sight of which warms your heart towards the whole world & softens into nothing the little troubles & vexations of life & the old enmities which have so long hung about our hearts are gradually dispelled by the cheerful blaze & soon forgotten. And as the fire burns higher & brighter & the hot ashes fall in great heaps—you form (in imagination) of them queer, fantastic shapes of men or huge Castles & then do the dear old castles in the air rise, and you build them still higher—& dream of bright, happy days—till,

Journal of a Hunting Excursion to Lewis Lake, 1851. Adirondack Museum, 1961.

like all day dreams, unfulfilled, a softening influence creeps over you—a strange forgetfulness—a drawing of your blanket closer & then—

The fish that had been saved over the night were frozen, so cold had been the air. After a hearty breakfast off of them we betook ourselves again to the river. Our success was "ravishing". For at least an hour we continued to draw out with our lines trout the largest & most beautiful we had ever seen. One in particular which the heavier body succeeded in landing— weighed over three pounds & according to the guides' statement—the largest he had seen that year but unfortunately from clumsy handling—he broke the hook from the snell & escaped. About 10 o'clk, our lines having become entangled in stumps, at the bottom, we were obliged to make such a stirring up of the waters that the fish became frightened & left & we followed their example. The lighter bodys line in particular had a great partiality for stumps & addicted itself to the same exclusively. We dined this day on *patridge & trout*—schgwpt!!! (an expression of delight. Don't your mouth water?) At 1 O'clock along came the expected wagon from Holmes', bearing the *boat* of the aforesaid Mr. Williams who did not arrive at the time appointed. Couch & Tim also came to join *us*—the boat, they were carrying in to Louis Lake. After a short consultation as to the best place for running deer, we concluded to shanty at Mason Lake three miles below Louis. We arrived here about sun-down & built ourselves a shanty of hemlock boughs in the woods. We built a roaring fire, cooked some pork—into which & the bread and butter we dove extensively & then went to sleep.

B.

(9th)

At six in the morning, having got everything in readiness, left Zulamee. Both men and beasts seemed much invigorated with the rest they had enjoyed, and at two in the afternoon reached Gundumowah, a small but neat Fellata village. The chief sent me a little milk.

(10th)

Early in the morning started for Sansanee. The country traversed was thickly wooded, and the path lay for three hours through a large bush, which, having recently been visited by a horde of elephants, the prints of whose feet were very perceptible, rendered travelling extremely unpleasant, and even dangerous. Reached Sansanee at one at noon. The site on which the town is built not being long cleared, none of the houses were quite finished. On our arrival, the chief had an open shed, occupied by fifteen calves, cleaned out for our reception. In the evening, putting the goods in the centre, I ordered the men to lie around them, whilst I placed myself near the most valuable articles. Not deeming them sufficiently secure, my sleep was rather dis-

Journal of the Second Expedition into the Interior of Africa from the Bight of Benin to Soccatoo, by Hugh Clapperton. Frank Cass Co, Ltd., 1966 (London). Orig. published 1829 by John Murray.

turbed; and awaking about ten o'clock, I found my camel had strayed from outside the hut, and being unwilling to arouse my drowsy companions, went myself in search of him. On my return, to my infinite surprise and alarm, discovered Pascoe had decamped, taking with him a valuable gun, two pistols, a cutlass, six sovereigns, nineteen dollars, ten large and ten small knives, and several other articles, which he had contrived to take from the boxes in which they had been placed. To deceive me, the artful old villain had put a pillow into a sack, which he had laid along on his own mat. On the discovery, I immediately made an alarm, and sent to the chief for twelve horsemen to go in pursuit of him.

(11th)

About three o'clock in the afternoon, as I was standing in my shed, I perceived a party of horsemen coming towards me in full gallop. On coming within a few yards of me, they suddenly checked their horses, and flourishing their spears over their heads, exclaimed, "Nasarah, acqui de moogoo!" (Christian, we have the rogue!) They informed me that a little before daybreak in the morning they heard the report of a gun, and going towards the place whence the sound seemed to proceed, saw Pascoe perched on the top of a high tree, and the stolen goods lying at the root of it. They threatened to shoot him with their poisoned arrows unless he immediately came down. This had the desired effect. He hastily descended, and delivered himself into their hands. One of the soldiers took the trembling scoundrel behind him on his horse, when the whole party immediately clapped spurs to their horses, and made all the haste they could to the village. I asked Pascoe what could have induced him to leave me in so disgraceful a manner. He replied that his countrymen (the Gooburites) were at war with the Fellatas, who would cut off his head on arriving at Soccatoo. The chief coming up at the instant, cried out, "A blessing, a blessing; you have taken the thief, let me take off his head!" This was Pascoe's third offence; and I ordered him to be heavily ironed and pinioned in the town dungeon.

- You probably haven't given any thought yet to what you'll want to leave to others when you die. Yet you're not too young to begin compiling the finest possible gift for unborn generations of your family. People inherit money, spend it, and it's gone; people who inherit journals treasure them always. Although a journal should be filled with *now*, it's really meant for forever. My great-grandfather was a faithful journal-keeper and lived a life filled with adventures. By the time he was an old man, his journals filled boxes. Then, the same week he died, my great-grandmother burned every one of them. No one ever figured out why. It still upsets me to think about it. How would you feel about such a loss?

- Journals are for storing stuff that's amusing:

(4/11/80)

Learned in science today that the vitamin was discovered by Casimir Funk. I think we should have a Casimir Funk Day every year.

(7/16/81)

Volunteer fire department report last month listed "two grass fires, one ambulance call, and one skunk removal."

(5/3/81)

Bing told me about an 81-year-old woman who used to go to revival meetings at church: "When she let out a whoop and jumped over three pews, you could tell the spirit had hit her."

(3/10/82)

Bobby can't stand the kid next door. He was splitting firewood the other day and the boy started taunting him. "Got so doggone mad I hit myself on the head with the go-devil. Swung her back and caught the doggone clothesline. Back she come and whacked me right on the skull." (A go-devil head weighs 8 pounds. The blow should've killed him.)

> "That made me so mad I did it again."
> "You mean *twice*?" I said.
> "Yup. Don't go tellin' anybody, but yeah, twice in a row."

- A journal's a good place to put resolutions too. You know what happens to most resolutions: we conveniently forget them. But put them in a journal and, like it or not, they don't go away. On paper, lying before you every time you page through your journal, a resolution seems much more like a contract between you and yourself than a half-remembered intention.

- Journals provide a way for people to talk to themselves on paper. There are times, though, when we don't want to "talk"—when filling the blank spaces with words seems a terrible effort. At times like these—and all journal-keepers experience them—the journal becomes a symbol of the self-discipline that all writers, you included, need. May Sarton, a poet and novelist, wrote this one day: "I have not felt like writing in this journal. It lies in wait each morning, and I long to put it off." (Notice that she wrote just the same.) Why should we write when we don't feel like writing? Not for practice. Not to prove that we're not lazy. And certainly not just to keep our journal entries neatly up to date. We should write because there's always something to discover, and the privacy of a journal provides the best place for finding out.

*   *   *

If you don't already keep a journal, start one today. Don't go out and buy one of those expensive things that looks like a hardcover book but is filled with blank pages. They don't lie flat and they're hard to write in. Start with a spiral or tablet-type notebook, and fill it with dreads and dreams and the deaths of rabbits. Keep it faithfully and don't stuff it full of showers and breakfasts, and when in ten years I offer you a thousand dollars for your stack of notebooks, you'll tell me to go jump in the lake.

At the same time, pick up a smaller notebook too, the kind you can fit in your pocket. It's for catching those small, sharp particulars that vanish almost as readily as they appear. It may take as little as 12 to 15 seconds to scribble enough of an impression so that your note will make sense that night or the next day. The pocket scribbler isn't meant to be filled with complete scenes, finished poems, or polished lines; it's for trapping fragments, whether they occur somewhere in the *outside* world: "Charlie says his brother hates his shadow"; or from somewhere *inside*: "My father's hands get angry before the rest of him." I can't say what of you belongs in such a scribbler, but something does, and daily.

A quite different function of a journal is connected directly with school. This kind of record is commonly called a "learning log," and according to most people who have kept them they're extremely useful. While the learning log isn't meant for capturing the random, unconnected fragments of life that only you experience, it *is* intended to be personal, to house only your thoughts and experiences. Nor is it meant to be graded. A learning log is a means for communicating with yourself and your teachers how you're responding to and understanding something you're studying.

It's not unusual for a teacher to meet with 150 students a day. Sometimes you can forget that, especially when the going gets rough—when you miss an important point under discussion or begin to hate a subject (or a teacher) because...well, just because. Few teachers think of students only as so many faceless lumps of humanity sitting in assigned seats. But it gets very difficult to deal with everyone on a person-to-person basis, to sense when a student is falling behind or losing interest. Sadly, this is when most students tend to clam up, and when that happens, even the most conscientious teacher can overlook those who most need to communicate with him. That's where the learning log comes in (although it's definitely not limited to times when there's a problem). It doesn't take more than five minutes to jot down in such a log your responses to a particular lesson or subject. Putting down what you think you've learned (or didn't) that day, whether it's in science or English or history, is an excellent way to make it stick, or to clarify a problem.

Class notes won't accomplish the same thing. Notes are usually taken without much thought; they're seldom summaries of anything; most of the time they're attempts to catch what the teacher has just said before she says something else. Here's what a class note usually looks like:

> Sonnet—14 lines. Iambic pentameter = each line 10 stresses, 5 iambs = 1 strong stress + 1 weak stress, example = *today, about, beware.* Shakespeare used iambic pentameter. Sample line = "Shall I compare thee to a summer's day?" Shakespeare's sonnets = 14 lines, 3 4-line stanzas and 2 lines at end with rhyming couplet.

Here's what a learning log entry, jotted down sometime after class, might look like:

Today Miss Nelson talked about the sonnet form of poetry. I don't really like poetry that much, especially when it's not modern. It seems harder to understand than prose, and most of the stuff we study in class is pretty old. I also wonder whether when Shakespeare wrote he expected teachers to pull his poems apart and make lessons out of them. The sonnet we studied today, for example. We never even got to the meaning of it—instead we learned about iambic pentameter, which is how many syllables fit in a line and where the accents are supposed to fall. I paid attention but I don't understand it. Does it have anything to do with rhyme? I'm afraid we'll have a quiz on it tomorrow. If we do I'm sunk. I realized something worrying about this, though. I read Sonnet 18 (Shakespeare numbered them) about 4 times and I began to know what it said. It's about someone so beautiful that there's nothing on earth to compare her with. I think I could put it in my own words. If the quiz is about what the poem means I'll be okay.

Or it might come out this way:

After class I read another poem, not Shakespeare, and I think it's in iambic pentameter. It was Robert Frost's "Mending Wall." It would be a good idea to use some poems like this that we know and have discussed to point out things like iambic pentameter. It's harder to learn about something when the wording of a poem is difficult too. Anyhow, I'd like to find out whether I'm right about Frost and iambic pentameter.

You can see how looking over such entries might benefit Miss Nelson. And you can also see how such a device might be helpful to you. Suppose a teacher read over your learning log once or twice a week and jotted responses to your comments and questions. What positive effects might this have on learning? In what class(es) in addition to English might such a log be useful to you? to the teacher? Are there advantages to one-to-one avenues of communication between student and teacher? Would a learning log make it easier for you to comment on matters that trouble you? excite you? Discuss these questions. Their answers could put you on to something that'll work for you not only now but for as long as you're a student.

*   *   *

The idea of a group journal may seem at odds with the rest of this chapter, but a journal in which more than one person enters a thought or experience can eventually become a treasure trove, especially if its contributors are family members. Such a journal, when it's left in some prominent place, begs to be read and written in. Now that you're acquiring the writing habit, why not urge it on others in the family too? The more I think about it, the more I wish that my family had made use of such an idea. It makes sense that if family members had a closer notion about how others in the same home felt and thought, people might avoid stepping on each other's toes so much. And that what might be awkward to say aloud might find its way into a family journal and please another. And that writing together could form a good, strong bond among the people we care about most.

Why don't you buy an inexpensive notebook, find a pen to go with it, write prominently on its cover something like "This is the _____ family journal, Volume One. Please put in it whatever is on your mind as you walk by. And don't walk off with the pen." Leave it in plain sight and make the first entry. Then watch what happens. (To avoid making what happens a disaster, don't use it as a gripe book. Its purpose is for sharing, communicating, not bellyaching or jotting down nastinesses you're afraid to utter aloud.)

When the ten minutes are up, take a look at what's on the paper. It may be just a list of random words, or even a ragged little essay on how foolish this experience seemed to you. The interesting thing is that something nearly always comes, whether or not you expect it to. Unplanned, nonstop bursts like this are called "free writing," and it's obvious why: when we let the pen move ahead of any organized thinking, we also leave behind much of what we've come to learn as writing rules, along with any worries about what words come out. And this creates a kind of freedom we're unused to (and even sometimes uncomfortable about). Such a release from the methods and responsibilities we've learned and long lived with can be rattling. It can also be misunderstood.

The term *free* may suggest that you're getting away with something, beating the system, slapdashing your way around the difficulties you connect with responsible, clear-headed writing. That's not the intent. These unplanned, uncomposed writings are a way to find out what's lurking in your mind at the moment, as well as demonstrating that writing doesn't always have to proceed from a conscious plan, an assignment we mull over and outline first. This book focuses on writing as an important way of *discovering*, squeezing into the narrow specifics of words and sentences the loose and unconnected swarms of ideas and images that flit about in your head and mine. People develop the notion that just by concentrating on an idea, problem, experience, they can organize these lightning bugs of thought into essay-like statements that can then be read with some kind of inner eye and written out. But can you do it? I can't. My mind is more like a magic slate than a computer. Let me *look* at what I'm thinking, though, even just a word or phrase, and there's a piece of it that can be fitted somewhere, that won't get bumped by a telephone ringing or the dog scratching to be let in.

Hurrying words onto paper will not magically make order, provide full answers, reveal in numbered frames what's inside. Only rarely will it result in a finished piece of writing. It will, however, give you something solid to look at and consider. It will make it much easier to forge a connection with something else. It will also provide surprises; often very powerful or funny stuff comes unplanned from your pen. Writing this way *loosens* too. Probably most of the writing you do is in and for school. If you're like most people, you've learned without being fully aware of it to write what sounds much like everybody else's writing—the kind that provides sensible answers to questions, fills up the required number of pages, earns a passing grade, does what's expected. Much school writing is stiff and empty, like a starched and ironed uniform standing at attention with nobody inside it. Part of the surprise that often occurs with unplanned, dashed off outpourings comes with finding a sentence or two that isn't stiff-sounding—that only you and not someone across the room could have written.

Whenever I've asked students to free write for the first time, at least half of them have said something like "Nothing happened," or "It was too stupid. I threw it away." Writers often judge themselves too harshly and quickly. Maybe nothing did happen; perhaps this particular ten minutes of

Then sometimes I just go with whatever hits me.

writing resulted in some hopelessly silly stuff. But there's also the chance that this kind of writing seemed so odd or bothersome that somewhere in the process you became convinced that nothing good would come of it. This is a normal response at first and usually goes away. Meanwhile, hold off on judging what did come. Resolve to delay judging any writing too early in its development. It's nearly always a mistake, one of the worst ones writers make.

Pencil manufacturers put erasers on one end of their product. This allows you to wipe out with one end what you created with the other. Except for the crumbs they leave, erasers are the perfect murder weapon, for they eliminate all traces of their victims. Indeed, that's the problem with having one on the end of your pencil. Early in any writing, erasing can be a mistake. Too often we murder words before we can possibly know that they won't make eventual sense, or trigger other words that will. By erasing we leave ourselves nothing to reconsider, re-see in other ways. Take a look at your pencil. If there's lots of lead left but almost no eraser, you're wearing out the wrong end first. Keep this in mind: *You can't change, improve, add to, even think about what's no longer there.*

People new to free writing sometimes dislike or misunderstand its results because they look at them the wrong way. As readers and writers, we get used to responding to whole pieces rather than individual lines. This works with finished writings such as essays, poems, and short stories, but it's the wrong way to deal with the results of a five- or ten-minute burst of words on paper. Usually there isn't much wholeness in this kind of writing (although there may be). More often it's a line or even just a phrase that has some promise; the rest may be junk. Thus, free writing requires a different kind of reading—more a weeding through than an overall scan. Here are some examples of free writing. Try reading them this way. If you were going to give each of these writers helpful advice, what lines would you single out as having possibilities? You're not necessarily looking for sentences that sound like beginnings of full-fledged essays; it may be just the poetic quality of a phrase or something faintly amusing or thought-provoking in a line. Look closely. Don't let any mechanical roughnesses interfere. Discuss your findings with others.

Rainbows Unicorns people doing nice things. Jenny B, Sandy my dog. My dead cow that I'm about to eat some steaks from tonight. Kathy F., the little girl I babysit down to the fish hatchery. Terry, Jesse, Danielles new house Homework. Too much homework—Pictures. The Bahama's Hawaii and the island with no electricity.

Jenny B.

Mowing the lawn with no shoes on. Walking in stubby grass. A two foot snake, on my foot. My feet turning green and cold. I move the mower back, the snake is headed straight for the blade. Now as I mow, I keep a watch for snakes.

Paula S.

Do you ever get the feeling when your in the elevator with a bunch of strange adults, that you're some little bug, that could be squashed under some fat woman's shoe? I do. I don't know what came over me to write this, but that's how I felt last night when I went to my cousin's apartment. It was as though I didn't exist. I was there but I wasn't. I was bodily there but I felt like I was somewhere else! Don't go thinking I'm on drugs or anything, because I'm not, and I never will be! It's just a thought.

Carolynn J.

To flow across
The blue-lined paper
With the slightest pressure
Of fingers guiding it along,
Being forced to use
The lead in its wooden shell.
Snapping the tip in two...
Then going to the sharpener
And filed
Only to be used again.

Martha B.

Here are some lines that other writers found after writing like crazy for ten minutes and weeding through the results. Try thinking about them as ways into longer pieces you'd enjoy reading.

The only thing I hate is watching birds migrate.

Today is just starting to wake up. It's getting buzzy with people and cars.

School looks the same as last year, but the bathrooms are painted a different color.

I hope Cinnicinate wins it all. I think I spelled Cinnicinate wrong.

We took the knives off the chopper yesterday and Grandpa is going to sharpen them.

It was nice to know that people all around came to help the couple whose house went down, and how the firemen worked all those hours free to make it safe, and how people do risk their lives to save animals.

Blue reminds me of little boys playing in a sandbox.

I used to be able to talk to her about anything that popped into mind.

When I go home I want to go fishing. The water will be very cold.

My heart stopped, or should I say it felt like it stopped? Then all of a sudden it started to beat really fast.

While I was thinking of something to write, my pen was writing already. But best of all it was writing my thoughts.

Whether or not you like these lines, each sounds as if it came from a specific *someone* rather than from a vague *anyone*. We can't judge the lines as being "good" or "bad," "right" or "wrong"; at this point they're only ways of holding on to an idea long enough to build on it or slide it into something else. Had they been overlooked, junked along with the maybe useless stuff that surrounded them, a possibly good start would have been lost forever.

Try to find a line or two from your own first free writing. Put what you find at the top of a page and do it again: free write under what you've found. Let what comes flow out of and around the stuff at the top. If nothing came the first time, try some more unplanned shotgunning. Something is bound to come. You're writing for yourself. Let any line take you wherever it will. You may like what begins to form enough to fuss with it (and title it, which can help)—to work it into something you'd like another to read. That's up to you at this point; for now the idea is to provide you with an experience that should reveal a use of writing you didn't know about before. Discuss with others what you think about this kind of experience, its possibilities, frustrations, surprises. Put what came out in your folder, not in the wastebasket.

Resolve to try the same thing tomorrow, even if it did no more than irritate you today. Free writing isn't a beginner's exercise. As a method for finding out what's going on inside, pushing yourself past the very natural urge to avoid writing, you should make free writing a permanent part of your writing life. Many writers rely heavily on it. If you keep at it it won't be long before its lasting value becomes clear to you.

*   *   *

In a book about Alaska called *Going to Extremes* by Joe McGinnis is a chapter about five men hiking through a partly unexplored and spectacularly beautiful stretch of the Brooks Mountain Range. One of the group, a National Park Service employee named Ray Bane, brought a notebook with him and often spent hours recording what he had seen. Once, after they had come upon a lovely meadow hemmed in by remarkable rock formations, the author noticed that "Ray Bane, who had seen so much, over so many years, was locked in an almost physical struggle to describe it." What took shape in his notes as the men sat there absorbing the scene was that it was like "being in the midst of a petrified thunderstorm."

This is a powerful way to describe the tortured shapes of rock, but what impressed me even more was why he bothered to enter this experience in a notebook—why he sat there and struggled: "I don't think a wilderness experience is complete," he told the book's author, "until it's been written about." If you take out the word *wilderness*, Ray Bane has stated the most important purpose for much of our writing—to complete experience. It isn't necessary to wait for a time when something spectacular happens to write it down. That's like walking around every day with a camera slung from your neck waiting for the right picture to present itself. Neither the writer not the photographer ever gets much good just waiting. The chances are that free writing will begin exposing to you experiences worth your struggling to complete. This unplanned writing is meant to give rough shape to thought; it isn't meant to begin and end in itself. You can't deal with all the possibilities that will present themselves, for there's enough swarming in your mind to fill libraries. But you can and should take some of what begins to form quite seriously, to understand that some of your discoveries *demand* completion.

This is where the "struggle" begins—where the writing becomes less "free." Often, young writers develop the notion that "If *I* can understand what I mean on paper, that's enough." Maybe. But I think this attitude is mostly a cop-out; I think it suggests that you really feel you don't have the talent for making an experience complete enough ("good enough") for others to share it. And there you're wrong. When was the last time you actually *struggled* to write something—fought an experience into what you and another reader might agree to be finished form? Ray Bane didn't struggle because he wanted an A on his notes. He simply took himself seriously enough to bother. He had developed enough faith in himself—not as a *writer* but as a *person*—to believe that capturing on paper what he experienced made a difference. If you take yourself seriously—if you write every day instead of waiting—you're going to find the same thing. If you're honest, you're going to be forced to admit that you're producing stuff worth bothering about, experiences worth completing.

Take just one of your lines and spend a few hours with it, this time not just to see where it leads you, but working intensely, "struggling" to make the image or experience sharp enough so that someone else can see it, experience it too. Never mind how long it turns out to be or what its subject is. Neither matters. What does matter is that taking your writing seriously amounts to taking yourself seriously, a connection you can't possibly appreciate without occasionally going through the almost physical battle to make things clear that Ray Bane went through. (If you want to see writers taking themselves seriously, visit an elementary school classroom.)

If you're uncertain about what line or lines to start with, ask other writers around you to respond to a few that you're considering. Find out which ones create the most powerful responses; then go from there.

4

How Long Should It Take?

Too often I wait for a sentence to finish taking shape in my mind before setting it down. It is better to seize it by the end that first offers itself, head or foot, though not knowing the rest, then pull; the rest will follow along.

André Gide

Poet William Stafford often sits alone early in the morning, before anyone else is awake, with a pencil and a blank piece of paper. "It's like fishing," he says. "But I don't wait very long, for there's always a nibble.... To get started I will accept anything that occurs to me. Something always occurs, of course, to any of us. We can't keep from thinking." Stafford recalls that when he first began to write about things he found in his world, "one thing would lead to another; the world would give and give." According to him, one doesn't become a writer because he has an extra-rich storehouse of things worth saying. A professional writer's world doesn't "give and give" any more than yours or mine. People don't need a special talent to become writers either, and as far as skills are concerned, Stafford believes that the only kind necessary to a writer "...is the skill we all have, something we must have learned before the age of three or four."

Here's an example of one young writer's "fishing," and what "nibble" she responded to. When she began, she had nothing more in mind than getting something, anything, on paper. She had no firm idea what it would become.

Cold – last night was even too much for the cat. He howled and came in stiff. So did the wind – I felt it – the cold on his fur. The wind made the ₍rooster on the₎ weathervane screech and howl like the cat and bent the apple tree. The cat, the weathervane, the apple tree – they were all moaning and screeching. Now the heat

24

makes noise. The radiator is hissing. It's the loudest noise I hear. The rooster on the weathervane is quiet. Maybe it froze overnight. When I walk outside the ground will crunch not like dry leaves but like walking on a broken light bulb. January = brittle, makes everything stiff, breakable. What's soft is only my white puffed breath.

Below is what she found. It took choosing; you can see that there are three or four other good possibilities. But this writer isn't wrong for going with this particular set of connections. Writing nearly always involves making choices, and most choices can be argued about. Maybe if this were your scribbling, you would have been pulled by the stillness of the morning or the broken lightbulb crunch of footsteps (I love that) or both. Consider this, however: what this writer has chosen *not* to deal with may eventually find its way into another piece. Attempts at discovering should never be thrown away. Tucked into a folder, they provide the writer's richest natural resource. Furthermore, we've looked at a piece of writing long before it was meant to go public. At this point the writer is not ready to say, "Here, read it, judge it. I think it's good enough to share."

*January is as (stiff as) the cat came coming in rubbing cold on? against my leg.
I think the weathervane rooster died overnight, froze to death, its bronze metal heart froze.
I heard its rusty screech when the cat came in. The apple tree moaned too. (?)*

Watch. She's choosing again:

I heard January spinning the weathervane rooster til it screeched and died. Stiff as January the cat came in rubbing cold winter on my leg.

We can't know yet exactly what she wants to find, but we're able to see movements toward something narrower, sharper. Her discovery is continuing:

The weathervane rooster, died froze last night
Its bronze heart froze at midnight. I heard
its screech when the cat came in as stiff
as January rubbing winter on my leg.

Eventually it led to this public poem (although looking back you can see that it could have ended up as either something else or nothing):

> The weathervane rooster
> Died last night.
> Froze its bronze heart in
> The spinning midnight
> Cold. I heard its last rusty screech
> When the cat came
> Stiff as January in the door
> Rubbing winter on my leg.
>
> *Terry K.*

(A couple of interesting notes: It wasn't January when she wrote, and she has no cat.)

Perhaps you're thinking, "Sure it's a good poem, but how long did it take her to write it?" The only reasonable answer to that question, although it may sound smartalecky, is "probably a lot longer than it would have taken to write junk." The "How long did it take?" question is very often asked by young writers exposed to a really good piece of writing by someone their age. But it really isn't so much a question as an observation in disguise. As a student you're given deadlines, often very tight ones, for most of your writing. You may be told on Friday to produce a two- or three-page composition by the following Monday. You're often expected to write a sensible essay in answer to a tough exam question in forty-five minutes. Under these conditions, one soon learns that to survive, writing fast is more important than writing well and that it's impossible to do both at the same time. Thus, when you ask "How long did it take?" you may really be saying, "I don't believe any normal student could knock out something like this under normal conditions." You're right, of course. Once in a while a writer gets lucky and can't do anything wrong, but mostly it's a long, wobbly struggle between first scribble and public piece.

Maybe I'll stir up trouble for you by saying this, but I believe that if you're honestly interested in writing, then it should be OK for you to say something like this about an assignment:

"I can't write about this. Please let me write about something else." Or, "I need more time to write about this the way I think it should be done." Or even, "I just can't write today; nothing's coming." Don't use any of those statements now, however. Get going on some writing instead of sitting there reading. You don't have to wait for tomorrow morning. If you stick with writing, you'll soon begin to sense that there's no such thing as a day off; that if you let 24 hours go by without involving yourself in some kind of writing, you'll feel faintly uncomfortable about it. (I admit, however, that if anyone had told me that when I was your age, I'd have fallen down laughing.)

For now, go back to your folder or your pocket scribbler. You'll find that looking back will occasionally provide a surprise, for words on paper have a way of changing when they're left in the dark. A line that might at the time have seemed silly or uninteresting may now seem attractive, worth working with. If neither of these sources yields anything, borrow Terry's idea about the sound of footsteps on frozen ground and see where that takes you. Writers borrow ideas from other writers all the time. It's not stealing.

Or write about what it's like to walk through an unfamiliar room in the dark, or the familiar sound of something banging against something else. Or wonder on paper about the sound of a siren. Or describe a photograph without looking at it. Or explain what it feels like to walk into a spider's web or wake up after surgery or hit somebody in anger or kiss a horse on its velvety muzzle or put a worm on a hook or why the names *January*, *February*, and *March* should be replaced with brighter, warmer names, or why you laughed when you should have cried. But no matter what you *begin* to write about, don't determine in advance that it's what you'll end up writing about. Think about what happened to Terry.

5

"No Ideas but in Things"

Even the best writer in his
best lines
is incurably imperfect....
Robert Lowell

The title above comes from a poem:

Compose. (No ideas
but in things) Invent!

In the poem, William Carlos Williams deals with a very difficult challenge for any writer: making see-able meaning with words. What do you think he means by "No ideas but in things"? Is it so simple and obvious a statement that all it deserves is a shrug and a "Sure, so what?" Stuck there between "Compose" and "Invent!" does it make clear these two essential, overlapping acts of writing? What does he mean by "thing" and "idea" anyhow? Use them for column headings and under them you could put everything in the world. (But don't try; you'd never finish.)

Between inventing and composing (or vice versa) is the need to find words that imitate the stuff of our minds. That may sound easy and natural, but it can be quite the opposite; it can be fiercely hard, not only for you and me but for the most brilliant writers. Words can never be the *ideas* they imitate. At best they can bring writer and reader fairly close in understanding. But no words, no matter how hard we labor to find the right ones, can make the understanding complete. Words are compromises. The struggle is to find the ones that compromise least, that come closest to the ideas we have in mind.

Why, then, didn't Williams say "No ideas but in *words*"? You can't put *things* on paper unless you draw pictures. Because he means, I think, that sometimes words, even the most carefully chosen ones, aren't enough. Not unless they bring to mind a *thing* that reader and writer already know together. The Williams poem offers readers a word that he trusted would bring to mind experiences and associations that he and they have shared in common. The word becomes a *thing* in that it pushes us past its narrow meaning and calls forth from our minds a burst of unworded ideas.

28

The thing in this poem is a snake. According to the dictionary, a snake is "a scaled reptile with a long, tapering body." But it wasn't this harmless string of words that terrified you years ago when a bigger kid chased you with one in his hand, or that startled you so powerfully when you mistook one for a stick. For most readers, *snake* produces a rush of wordless feelings ranging from fascination to terror. And when that happens, *snake* ceases to be a *word* and becomes the thing, stirring up in us reactions we do not find in dictionaries. Look how Williams uses *snake* to let us know his idea:

> Let the snake wait under
> his weed
> and the writing
> be of words, slow and quick, sharp
> to strike, quiet to wait,
> sleepless.

Shouldn't words strike like a snake sometimes? Dart out and shock us? Send a cold shiver up our spines? Pull back, quiet and hidden, and then when we least expect it, strike again? *Snake*, as Williams uses it here, has the power to make us react strongly, first with the jolt that snakes cause when we happen on them unexpectedly; then with an understanding that, yes, this is what writing can do too. Take the snake out and what happens?

> Let the writing
> be of words, slow and quick, sharp
> to strike, quiet to wait,
> sleepless.

The message is still there, but not the jolt, the surge of images and recollections triggered by "snake." We understand, but perhaps less clearly or eagerly.

Read this next poem by William Carlos Williams two or three times. See if you can find in it further evidence about what the poet means by "No ideas but in things."

> *The Red Wheelbarrow*
>
> so much depends
> upon
>
> a red wheel
> barrow
>
> glazed with rain
> water
>
> beside the white
> chickens.

What do you see and feel after this reading? Jot down a quick list of things besides the wheelbarrow and the chickens. (One student, for example, saw "an upside-down washtub drummed by the rain.") How many chickens are there? Where are you? Looking out a rain-streaked window? Peering through a hole in a fence? What time of day is it? Are you alone? happy? sad? How old are you?

That many readers of this poem have no trouble providing quick, clear responses to questions like these suggests that, like the snake, the wheelbarrow and the chickens in the rain are together a powerful image that sparks our imaginations in ways we can't quite explain but that probably has little to do with "a small vehicle with handles and one or more wheels for carrying small loads" and a few "common domestic fowl." (Try substituting *mailbox* or *lunchpail* or *washtub* for *wheelbarrow*. What happens?)

Why does Williams say that "so much depends upon" this thing of words? If for a moment what you see beyond his words brushes what he sees, a small miracle has taken place. Maybe much of what we write should begin with the invisible words "so much depends upon..."

Does a "thing" form for you that much depends upon? an idea or image that will perhaps stir up associations in another? Try this: put the line "so much depends upon" on a blank piece of paper and see if it pulls anything from you. Here is what three young writers found:

> so much depends
> upon
> mud oozing
> between my toes
> after
> a warm rain.
>
> *Mary D.*

> so much depends
> upon
> a little
> blue bike.
>
> *Ann H.*

> so much depends
> upon
> my black doberman
> catching
> an orange frisbee
> in mid-air.
>
> *Roger H.*

You can't tell whether or not your words amount to the kind of "thing" Williams talks about unless you offer your writing to others and get their reactions. In response to your writing, ask several classmates to jot down, much as you did, what your words trigger in them—the images and associations your writing may call forth. An alternative to this is to ask them to sketch a picture of what they see. This doesn't require artistic talent; even stick figures will reveal whether what you saw as you wrote resembles at all what listeners saw when they read.

What all this "No ideas but in things" discussion boils down to is the simple truth that if you write to make something clear for yourself, there's a good chance that you'll make it clear to someone else. A temptation all writers must turn away from is putting loosely, vaguely, the vivid images and ideas that live inside you. Lines like "Autumn is a really beautiful season" or "I think little kids are wonderful" may be okay if they lead into some specifics that allow both you and someone else to see and know what you mean. Often, though, it stops here, because the writer is lazy or hurried or simply doesn't mean very deeply what he says. People also have the mistaken belief that as long as the ideas exist sharply inside, writing them out accurately and honestly is a troublesome waste of time. Little in memory stays sharp. At least occasionally when something touches you, wrestle it into words as close to the something as possible. Otherwise, you'll probably lose it for good. These short samples of young people's writing caught something before it got away:

> The silver-backed fish swimming along with me look like pieces of glittering glass shining under water.
>
> *Deo J.*

> Early in the morning when I check my traps and see the highlights of a fox's ears, it seems a shame to kill for money.
>
> *Dan K.*

> I look out the window
> To watch
> The wind
> Blow petals off flowers.
> As innocently
> As life began,
> A stem breaks.
>
> *Martha B.*

> Sitting on the Ford tractor I feel its power. I stop. My body is numb from the rough ground. I sit with the heat beating down.
>
> *Randall H.*

Your turn: "Compose. (No ideas but in things) Invent!" What did you see today that no one else noticed? Even now as you look around, what catches your eye? Surprises? What looks different to you now than it looked when you were six? What, if you were able to do so, would you most like to capture—a scene like the one Williams caught? The feel of something rough under your hand? A smell that always brings a sharp memory to mind? An apple core and a pickle on a paper plate? The way someone moves, speaks, stretches, yawns? Three birds sitting on a telephone wire in the rain? For all of us, so much depends on matters like this. Go catch one. Say as simply and directly as you're able what it is. Keep at it; good writing can start in a rush, but finally becomes a slow struggle to say it so others can know it too.

I've heard at least fifty young writers say about "The Red Wheelbarrow," "There's nothing to it at all. Anybody could have written it." I wouldn't be surprised to learn that Williams had spent a month on it. Often the toughest part of writing is saying it simply, so don't get discouraged if what first comes isn't quite simple and clean enough. Keep at it. Remember that if good writing were as easy as it sometimes appears to be, the world would be so stuffed with it that we wouldn't value it at all.

6

Ossferious Slugs

No chant — This is a story starter

Inside this pencil
crouch words that have never been
written
never been spoken
never been thought....

W.S. Merwin

Take a look at this collection of odd beasts, but don't discuss with others how they look to you, what you think they resemble or bring to mind. Instead, try writing about them without anyone else's inspirations to guide you. I've done something on the first one, mostly for my own amusement. Accompanying the rest of the menagerie are other writers' responses. If you can't seem to find a way at first, consider these possibilities (but don't feel bound by them): Where does it sleep? What does it eat (besides goldfish)? How would your parents react to your bringing one home for the weekend? Where would you be likely to find one? How would you feel if you woke up and found that you had turned into one overnight? If it were an endangered species, would you worry about its loss or about its possibly surviving and multiplying? Who would you most like to give one to for Christmas? Do something on each of them, including the ossferious slug, and make sure to name them all. When you're done, swap your responses with someone else and someone else after that.

These are ossferious, perambulous slugs,
Who'll slide down your chimney and hide under rugs.
Count the goldfish each morning.

33

If you miss one or two,
Or the parakeet's gone
Without leaving a clue,
Do what you want,
But I know what *I'd* do.
I'd hide in the attic
Or move to Peru,
Because sooner or later they'll come looking for you.

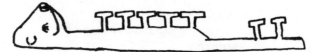

This creature is a typing tiger (scientifically *typus tigrus*), which blends into its surroundings: typewriters or computers with keyboards. Rarely seen or heard, it leaves little indication of its presence, except perhaps a half-eaten ribbon. The typing tiger has a notoriously short temper, is vicious, and bites off the fingers of unsuspecting typists. Secretaries are the most common victims.

The typing tiger enters a typewriter as a minute bacteria. It grows on ink and typing ribbon, and as it matures (to about twelve inches) it invades the keyboard. Here it builds a nest and hatches its young. During this period it is extremely protective and is apt to eat a finger or two. Most creatures don't like to be poked and have to babysit at the same time.

If your typewriter or computer is acting strangely, investigate. A typing tiger may be at hand.

John G.

Today I took a happy hike
And wandered lovely trails
Until by accident I fell
Upon a bed of nails.

John S.

(Another young writer labeled this smiling beast a "saxaphone slug," and let it go at that. I had never even considered this delightful possibility, even though I drew the sketch.)

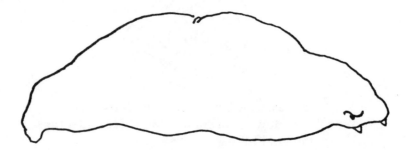

Water stumbles over it;
An obstruction in its path.
Like a shiny cake of soap, glowing
Red from the heavy evening sun,
Under the cliffs it lies,
Snoring the songs of dreams.

Julie V.

It isn't the fangs and frown that bother me. It's the way this fat, shape-less creature would be slumbering in some dark place, and I'd touch it reaching for some familiar thing, or even worse I'd feel it under my bare foot, something dead but warm.

Kelly C.

Did you ever wonder what makes
The whistling voice
That everyone says
Is just the wind?

Jim J.

This odd fellow is a cross between a coat-hanger and a tree sloth.

Dale C.

It's easy to see why he doesn't let go.
He's afraid to stub his only big toe.

Helena R.

Create an ossferious slug or two of your own. Get copies made, enough for four or five people or perhaps the entire class. When you get their versions back, be sure to tell them what your beast *really* is, so they won't go away confused. The results, along with the pictured creatures they describe or comment on, should definitely be collected, displayed, and bound in some permanent form.

7

Remembering

Assemble first all casual bits and
scraps
That may shake down into a world
perhaps....

Robert Graves

When I was seven I climbed the steep, narrow stairs to my grand-mother's attic for the first time. The roof was low and sloping, and the light from the small window and the single bulb did not reach into the dark, musty-smelling corners of the room. That was where I found the treasures that drew me back up those stairs again and again until I had played and read and wound and worked all the dusty relics of boy-hood my three uncles had outgrown and left there at least twenty years before.

I remember putting to my lips an old trombone and tasting the sour brass of its mouthpiece, and taking back down with me one summer morning a catcher's mitt so cracked and stiff it was beyond use; and a box of mysteries and westerns and a book on magic tricks and another on cartooning. I found a football with a gray rubber bladder that in-flated by mouth and a pair of funny-looking shoulder pads and the kind of leather helmet you see in old newsreels of Red Grange. There were model airplanes with fragile balsa-wood ribs covered with stif-fened paper, and a dartboard so full of holes that the bull's-eye was chewed out, and two tennis rackets, both warped and unstrung, and.... I could list a hundred other things, all of them fascinating and useless, all left the way you put something down when you plan on coming back to get it again. Then I grew too old for them too and came down the stairs one day and did not ever climb them again.

About thirty years later, though, when almost all the people who had lived in my grandmother's house were either dead or moved away, I called the one old uncle who lived there still and said, "Up in the attic under the eave on the north side of the house there's a banjo. Okay if I borrow it?"

"Hang on a minute," he said, "I'll see if it's still there." Maybe five minutes later he came back to the phone. "It was right where you fig-ured," he said.

I drove a hundred miles that night because I couldn't wait to feel it in my hands.

I just wrote this little piece. I sat down, not really sure what I meant to say, and from a corner of my mind as dim and cluttered as my grandmother's attic I discovered a scrap—not a complete idea, just a scrap—and put it down. It was like finding part of my uncle Vin's trombone and not knowing what it was but figuring it was something that probably went with something else.

That's how writing often gets started, with a scrap of something that has a shape or sound that makes you want to fit it with something else once you see it on paper. This piece started with the scrap "banjo in the attic," which suggested that the writing would deal with my remembering that old instrument, getting it and fixing it up so it would play. But instead I got drawn into memories of the attic itself, and as I scribbled on, they took over, swinging me away from the earlier idea. If this were an essay exam, such wandering would be dangerous, but when you're writing for yourself, dealing with feelings and experiences only you have had, it's OK to go where the writing seems to be leading. This isn't the time to worry about order either. Memory isn't like a file cabinet, with everything neatly arranged. It's usually a jumble, and jotting things down gets the jumble outside, makes it less fuzzy.

When you see a writer looking out the window with her pen poised above the paper, she's probably trying to write a sentence or even an entire piece in the air. This kind of "writing" is often the result of believing that you must know exactly what you want to say before you say it, and that until the perfect sentence comes, it's a mistake to put anything on paper. This can lead to paralysis or bad writing. It also drains any pleasure out of the experience. You shouldn't be bullied by a fear of making mistakes. Get something, anything, on paper instead of waiting for the perfect words to write themselves on a window pane or the ceiling. There's usually no way to tell at first whether something's right or wrong, anyhow. The important issue is whether or not the line *works*, and you can't make any decisions about that until you've tried it out with other lines and finally with other readers. Writer Peter Elbow tells his readers, "First make a mess." It's good advice.

Cleaning up the "mess"—shaping the loose pieces into a form that pleases the writer—is the most satisfying aspect of writing. We have a natural urge to do this, to imitate our "ideas" with the "things" of words. Forming isn't just a final fixing or dressing up. It starts when the writing starts and continues through the process. Moving, changing, and discarding are ways of seeking form. They represent experiments, not corrected mistakes. The urge to form is also connected with the need to make a piece of writing ours—to put our personal stamp on it, especially when it deals with a personal subject. The forms you and I favor will be different, and so will our ways of arriving at them. Here's a sample from my mess. You can see how things got shuffled and thrown out; and if you look back, you can also see that still more changes happened before the final version formed.

~~I can remember~~ my grandmother's attic from [when I was seven or eight] *I used to visit*

~~And used to~~ *to* play there on rainy days. The stairs were narrow

and the roof sloped, *was low and* ~~There was only~~ *The* one small window and *a* single

~~light~~ *b* bulb, ~~and the light did~~ *enough to* not reach into the dark, musty corners.

gave off some light, but ~~That was where~~ *remember an* I ~~found the~~ *finding* old trombone and put it to my lips and *ring*

tasted *ing* the sour dust on the mouthpiece. There was a catcher's mitt

too, so cracked and dry that when I took it back downstairs I could

useless see that it was beyond use. [Everything in the attic was like that--

the way things from another time are. stiff and old-smelling, belonging to another time.] ??

Discuss what you agree or disagree with here. What changes seem necessary? Which ones may have made the section worse rather than better?

*   *   *

Here's a memory piece from a young writer. Tom wrote his first version quite rapidly, and it shows. It's bumpy and filled with errors, almost as if its author were still the little boy with the broken helmet and the broken heart.

> When I was a little boy my parents gave me a red fire chiefs helmit. This helmit was briliant red with gold plastic ear muffs. It had a golden eagle sticker on the forehead of the helmit. This helmit was special, it had a microphone with speakers in the ear muffs. I played with the helmit for three days. On the third day my father thought he would try this toy. Because the helmit was meant for a child he broke it. I was heart broken, and never got another fire chiefs helmit.

What counted at this point, though, was that Tom got out on paper a moment that had lodged in his memory for years. Now he was able to look at it. (It's extremely hard to see a long-ago memory clearly without getting it on paper.) The second version was not just an attempt to "fix" the first one—to correct mechanical errors. Here, the author has looked at a part of himself caught in writing and has attempted to make the picture sharper, closer to the experience itself. (He fixed up most of the mechanical errors too.)

> When I was a little boy, about five or six, my parents gave me a red fire chiefs helmet. It was only a toy. This helmet was brilliant red with gold colored plastic ear muffs. It had a sticker in the form of a golden eagle. The helmet was special, it had a microphone with speakers in the ear muffs.
>
> I played with this helmet for three days consistently. On the third day my father thought he would try this toy. Because the helmet was meant for a child, it would not fit an adult, and my father broke it. I was

heart broken, and never got another fire chiefs helmet. My father said it was too cheap, it broke so easily.

Notice that the writer has added three pieces of information that seemed important to him: he was "about five or six," he was so thrilled with the helmet that he played with it "consistently," and his father never considered how important the helmet was to his small son. These additional details are important for the reader too. They help us remember more sharply what it was like to be a helpless five- or six-year-old in a world of clumsy, thoughtless adults.

The chances are that Tom began to consider in the second version how others would react to the piece. Consider how often in conversation we eagerly share such experiences as this, either to amuse or make an important point. Much talk comes out in *narrative form*, story-like exchanges that often begin, "When I was...." or "I remember the time...." In this respect, writing and talking are the same; both are based on the natural human need to be listened to, accepted, believed. Just as important, both provide ways for us to reexamine the thoughts and experiences that make each of us different from everyone else. Had Tom been writing only for himself, the first version probably would have been good enough.

Notice that the third version is more polished (or "mature"-sounding) than the previous ones. The writer has moved his memory into a form that satisfies him, gets closer to what he wants it to be, and also closer to how he wants to be known as a writer in this instance.

When I was five or six my parents gave me a toy fire chiefs helmet. It was brilliant red with gold colored plastic ear muffs. Inside the helmet there was a microphone with speakers in the ear muffs and on the front was a gold sticker shaped like an eagle. For three days I played with it constantly. On the third day my father thought he would try it. Because the helmet was meant for a child, it would not fit him and he broke it. Then he said it was cheap because it broke too easily. I was heart broken and never got another helmet.

Discuss whether you agree with Tom's final choices. Don't just generalize; examine the particulars. Would a fourth version possibly have been better? It isn't hard to spot weaknesses here that might have been eliminated with more revision. But keep in mind too that no piece of writing is ever truly perfect, and that even though you as a writer will never feel entirely satisfied with what you've put on paper, there comes a time when any writer must say, "I'm done; it's good enough." As for this memory piece being good enough, consider how Tom's father might feel if he read it today.

Inside you is a world you know deeply and strongly. You can bring it out to look at and share, small pieces at a time. Try now. Begin with a single memory and simply begin writing. Let anything spill out. No timed writing this time; keep going until you sense that there's enough on paper to make some choices about. Obviously, I can't provide a list of your memories to get you started, but here are broad possibilities that should suggest some specific recollections. You're not, of course, limited to any of these.

- a thoughtlessness or cruelty you'll never forget, not only because it continues to stir a guilt in you, but because somehow it was also a part of growing up, of discovering that Santa Claus and Mother Goose eventually get replaced by harsh realities.
- a special place where you and friends gathered to play and in which you imagined yourselves, when you were small, to be participants in great and dangerous adventures.
- a frustration that, like Tom's, was specific proof that a child has fewer rights and oftentimes vastly less importance than older people.
- a friend you knew you'd have forever and whom you never see or hear from anymore.
- what you see when you close your eyes and bring forth a picture for the thousandth time that makes you know that your family is at its best closer than most.
- what once terrified you but now seems silly or harmless.
- the way your grandfather or grandmother made something, did something, expressed anger or amusement or affection.

Make a mess. Add stuff. Throw stuff out. Keep making connections. Push the pieces around until you feel and see a form coming. In other words, clean up the mess.

The best way to find out if a piece of writing works is to show it to someone else, the way you might show a friend a photo of a place or person he couldn't otherwise know. When you show another person something you've written, you'll be tempted to fill him in, to say something like, "This is really what I meant to say," or "Let me explain what I meant by that." Don't. Keep quiet. Leave your reader alone. Then ask what he thought of it. Find out if he saw and heard and smelled what you did. Be fair to yourself, though: good writing can come somewhere near to the experience, but no writer can make it *be* the experience. So don't judge yourself too harshly if your reader doesn't get it exactly.

*   *   *

Here are a couple of memory pieces by young writers. They're good, but probably not better than what you'll produce if you stick at it. I watched both writers develop these pieces from the first uncertain push of the pen. According to them, neither knew at the start where the writing would go, but within a half-hour or so, both had filled a couple of pages with "messes." Finally, after a few days of hashing things around, this is what came:

It was the first time I ever shot anything. I was about nine years old. A friend and I were walking down a dark street. Mike had his bee-bee gun. As we got closer to a streetlight we could see a shadow racing through a pile of trash. When we reached the rim of the light's rays, Mike recognized it as a small cat. It was playing with a ball of aluminum foil.

Mike, who was used to shooting things, pumped the gun five or six times and took careful aim. A couple of seconds later the cat was lying on the ground squirming and meowing. Mike laughed as he watched the dying cat. I felt sorry for it. Although it was a stray, I didn't think it deserved this pain.

Mike handed me the gun: "Here, finish it off. Then we'll go find something else to shoot at."

As I took the gun from his hands, he told me how to use it. "Find the cat's head in the triangle at the end of the barrel. Then pull the trigger and Pow! Dead cat."

I stared at the cat while he explained the directions. I raised the gun, found the cat's head. My hands started to sweat as the trigger moved under the pressure of my finger. I closed my eyes. The gun went off. I heard a sickening noise. The cat let out its last cry. When I opened my eyes, Mike had it, holding it in the air by its tail. Blood dripped from its head.

"Right through the head. Good shot. Now let's go find something else."

"I have to go home," I said, so we left. When we reached my house, he suggested shooting at cans.

"Good night" was all I said.

Jeff C.

I remember when our family used to live in South Kortright. We owned a small farm that held about forty cows. We called it Betty Brook's Farm because it was the oldest place on Betty Brook Road.

I used to help my dad, no matter what he did. I was always with him. Sometimes he let me drive the tractor. I was only six but Dad sat me on his lap. The throttle was up high on the steering column so I could regulate it. I even shifted, but Dad had to work the brake and clutch. My legs were much too short for that.

I drove the John Deere with the manure spreader out from the manure tunnel under the barn, across the old dirt road, and through the gate into the pasture. I went very slowly and never once hit the gate post. The days after a rain I let Dad drive because I loved to watch the big rear wheels slowly swish the muddy water from the puddles. It made little waves swim to the edges, as the wheels sliced it in two.

Then we went up the hill and rode along the brow. It always scared me. I could picture the tractor tipping and rolling over and over down the steep slope. But Dad always told me it was just a little hill, even though it looked huge to me.

We never tipped over, of course. And no matter how scared I was back then, I always enjoyed the ride.

Lisa C.

These pieces are included here for a couple of reasons. You can get so wrapped up in the study of writing that it becomes some kind of end in itself; its real purposes are forgotten. Discuss the following—and take the discussing seriously: would you be surprised to find Jeff's or Lisa's piece in a literature book? Why or why not? Can you think of reasons why writings that come out of your own class (including your own work) would be appropriate to study as "literature" instead of being looked at only as "writing" for writing study's sake? Does writing have to be "professional" to be worth reading and discussing and learning from? Consider how the writing that happens in your class might be fitted into what we classify as "literature study."

But let's not neglect immediate concerns either: finding out how writing works for you and others in your class. Look at Jeff's fifth paragraph. As he relived his memory, forced it into writing, something about that sickening few seconds must have suggested to him that those tight, rapid-fire lines would convey the tension he felt. From the sentence "I closed my eyes" to "The cat let out its last cry," the reader is squeezed into the situation too. In a different way, Lisa's third paragraph does the same thing. It's like the progress of the tractor, slow-moving, lumbering along in low gear. And the last two sentences in the paragraph seem almost to "slowly swish," making the puddle crossings beautifully seeable. Lines like this move an experience past locked-away memory into forms that allow others to share it. They don't always come easily, and they're seldom a matter of luck. But to find them doesn't take special talent or A grades in English. We all have a sense about language that has developed over the length of our lives, a way of knowing when our words begin to capture the images within our minds. We look at a line and say, "No, that doesn't say it," or "This doesn't belong here," and if we care, we find a better way.

Why bother? I can't explain it exactly, but for Jeff it came out in the comment, "I never thought I could do it." He had discovered that he was a writer, and that is like discovering anything else deeply worthwhile and satisfying about yourself. But I think Jeff was also referring to having found there on paper a moment of his life that a week ago was only a fuzzy fragment and now was sharp and permanent.

8

Fabling

An old hen will put up with anything if you'll give her a little affection now and then.

(The moral of "The Fisherman and the Hen")
William March

A fable is a short, short story, usually with animals for characters. At the end of most fables is a moral. Here are four fables. I've left out the morals for the last two.

Once there was a mother crab who had a small son. One day she said to him, "Son, I wish you would learn to walk properly. You look so foolish and clumsy scuttling along sideways. It's time you began walking straight and properly."

"Sure thing, Mom," the young crab said. "Just show me how to do it and I'll follow right along."

Moral: *It's usually foolish to expect of others what you yourself cannot provide.*

A lion lay sleeping in his den when a small mouse, not realizing its mistake, ran across the lion's nose and woke him. The angry lion caught the mouse under his huge paw and prepared to put an end to it. The mouse pleaded for its life, however, and the lion, who was not a bad sort, decided to spare the tiny creature.

Not long after, the lion became hopelessly tangled in a snare set by hunters. In his anger and fear he let out a roar that shook the forest. The mouse heard it, scurried to where the lion lay helpless, and quickly chewed through the knots that held the lion captive.

Moral: *Kindness is seldom wasted, whether it comes from the meek or the mighty.*

A donkey worked for a kindly master, who fed and watered him well, provided a clean stall and never asked him to carry a heavy load. Nevertheless, the donkey wasn't satisfied with his treatment. What especially annoyed him was that the master's little dog, who did nothing at all to earn his keep, lived in the lap of luxury, eating the finest leftovers from its master's plate, curling up on his lap, and sleeping by the fire on chilly nights. None of this sat well with the donkey, and he resolved to earn the same comforts.

One day at dinnertime, he kicked open the door of his stall, trotted across the barnyard and pushed his way into his master's house. Once inside he began to leap about and bray, mimicking what he thought to be the antics of a playful dog. Finally, after knocking over the dinner table and upsetting most of the furniture, he leaped upon his astonished master's lap. That, needless to say, did it. The master and his servants dragged the donkey from the house, beat it severely and turned it out to pasture far from its comfortable stall.

Moral:

A butcher once tossed a juicy scrap of meat to a hungry-looking stray dog. The dog, who had not eaten for many days, snatched it up in his jaws and ran off with it, determined to devour it in peace, far from any other dogs who might attempt to take it from him.

His route took him across a bridge that spanned a small stream. Halfway over he noticed his reflection in the water. What he thought he saw mirrored below him was another dog, this one too with a piece of meat in its jaws. At that moment an ancient truth known to all dogs occurred to him: There is nothing better in life than a piece of fresh meat, unless it is two pieces. With that truth firmly in mind, he opened his jaws to growl, thinking to frighten his reflection into dropping its morsel. What happened, of course, is that his scrap fell into the stream and was gone.

Moral:

You've noticed, I'm sure, that morals are advice. Not for animals who, as you know, don't pay the slightest attention to advice. (It would be a waste of time to tell a hen that she shouldn't count her chicks before they're hatched.) Morals are pieces of advice for people (who often, like hens, pay no attention to them). They apply to countless situations. Do you have a favorite fable, complete with moral? Most people do. Because they're short and have simple story lines, fables are easy to remember. They also tend to stick in our memories because their morals seem to fit so many situations and people. Some fables have been told and retold so often that they have woven themselves into our language and no longer have to be repeated in full for us to recognize. The Volkswagen company ads refer to a new model as "a wolf in sheep's clothing" because they know that the words will remind readers of a particular fable. What story comes to mind when you hear someone's behavior described as "sour grapes"? What's the fable behind the statement "You shouldn't cry wolf"? What kind of person would be described as "a dog in the manger"?

Provide morals for the two fables above. You may want to jot down more than one for each. It isn't necessary to use the somewhat formal language often found in morals. Just put in your own words a piece of advice that applies to you and me. ("Donkeys shouldn't jump on people's laps" may be perfectly true, but it isn't very useful.) Truth is often easier to swallow if it's on the humorous side. Here's a fable by American humorist James Thurber. (It's from his book *Fables for Our Time*, which you should definitely read.) Jot down three of four possible morals that could fit this fable. In keeping with the tale itself, they should be humorous. But they should also contain a truth of sorts that goes beyond the circumstances of fable. (Thurber's moral is on p. 49, but don't look at it until after you've shared and discussed the ones you've devised.)

The Bear Who Let It Alone
James Thurber

In the woods of the Far West there once lived a brown bear who could take it or let it alone. He would go into a bar where they sold mead, a fermented drink made of honey, and he would have just two drinks. Then he would put some money on the bar and say, "See what the bears in the back room will have," and he would go home. But finally he took to drinking by himself most of the day. He would reel home at night, kick over the umbrella stand, knock down the bridge lamps, and ram his elbows through the windows. Then he would collapse on the floor and lie there until he went to sleep. His wife was greatly distressed and his children were very frightened.

At length the bear saw the error of his ways and began to reform. In the end he became a famous teetotaller* and a persistent temperance lecturer. He would tell everybody that came to his house about the awful effects of drink, and he would boast about how strong and well he had become since he gave up touching the stuff. To demonstrate this, he would stand on his head and on his hands and he would turn cartwheels in the house, kicking over the umbrella stand, knocking down the bridge lamps, and ramming his elbows through the windows. Then he would lie down on the floor, tired by his healthful exercise, and go to sleep. His wife was greatly distressed and his children were very frightened.

Now that you've had the opportunity to examine the shape and function of the fable, it should be an amusing challenge to write one or two of your own. If you like, use the familiar characters that keep popping up in well-known fables: the wolf, the lion, the fox, the goat, the donkey, the camel, the stork, the peacock, the rooster, for example. And perhaps their familiar qualities too: wolves are always out to devour some weaker species; foxes use their wits to fill their stomachs; lions rely on their frightening size and strength to get their way; donkeys nearly always play the fool; storks (or cranes) take advantage of their wit and long beak to win the day; and peacocks and roosters are silly and vain by turns. However, there's no good reason why you shouldn't ignore these well-known characters and circum-

teetotaller: a person who doesn't drink alcoholic beverages.

stances in favor of fresh ones. I have never read fables featuring kangaroos or beavers, for instance, and it seems a shame that such animals have been overlooked.

Whatever the characters and circumstances of your fable(s), keep the story brief and simple, and let it be a clear example of any of these morals:

1. It's best to let well enough alone.
2. Persuasion works better than force.
3. Or use the moral in the headnote.

If none of these morals triggers an idea for a fable, substitute your own. Again, keep in mind that it should be a general kind of truth, one that will apply and be useful in a variety of circumstances.

Most of our favorite fables have come to us from Aesop, a Greek who lived about 2500 years ago. You might have a copy of *Aesop's Fables* at home, and certainly your school or public library has one. After 25 centuries of controlling the fable market, it's time that old Aesop had some competition. Why not put together and publish the collected fables produced by you and your classmates? Because they're short, fables are easy enough to reproduce in finished, typed form for copying. Each of you should have a booklet for your own, and of course the library should have one too.

*   *   *

Life's lessons often come in story form, although not necessarily through fables. Each of us as we mature develops a collection of private tales that, because they're based on personal experience and have taught us something valuable about life, we think about and tell and retell to make or strengthen a point. Often a well-told story from someone's personal experience can be the best way to offer advice. Russian writer Anton Chekhov used to tell a story about an uncle to whom someone gave a kitten. The uncle wanted it to become a champion mouser, so while the kitten was still very young, he showed it a caged mouse. But the kitten, whose hunting instincts hadn't developed yet, showed only slight interest in the mouse. The uncle felt that the kitten hadn't demonstrated the right spirit, so he scolded it, slapped it, and chased it away from the cage.

The next day he repeated the lesson. This time the kitten showed some signs of fear when it was placed next to the cage. And again the uncle responded the same way, striking and shouting at the kitten. The lesson was repeated day after day for some time, and each day the kitten grew more frightened and the uncle grew angrier. After a few weeks, whenever the kitten was brought near the mouse it shrieked in fear and tried to run away. Finally, the uncle got so disgusted he gave the kitten away, determined that it was the stupidest cat in the world. This wasn't the case, of course; the cat was anything but stupid. It had learned its lesson well, although it wasn't the lesson the uncle intended. Chekhov used to end the story with this comment: "I can sympathize with that kitten. The same uncle tried to teach me Latin."

This isn't a fable (although it has certain fable-like qualities). It's a story that came out of Chekhov's personal experience. On the personal level, it's a simple tale about a harsh uncle and an unfortunate kitten that happened to fall into his hands. But that's not why Chekhov often told the story, as amusing as it is. The story makes a useful point, not just about an uncle and a kitten. Discuss what that point is. What is there in this tale that applies to all of us? How would we respond to such a form of education?

Write up your own version of how someone's attempting to teach a lesson backfired. What Chekhov's story brought to mind for me was my training my first horse to rear up on its hind legs, the way movie cowboys' horses did. It didn't take her long to figure out that if she reared up high enough I'd fall off and she could then trot back to the barn rather than carrying me around. It took me six months and many bruises to unteach her. Perhaps you've made a similar mistake. But your story needn't involve animals, nor does it have to be first-hand. If you can't think of a "teaching" blunder you've made or that involved you directly, certainly you've heard someone else recount such an experience, and probably you've remembered it because it contained a lesson about life. Write it up and share it. Discuss these stories the same way you did Chekhov's tale.

What other sorts of experiences do you tell about in story form to make a point about:

- being so egotistical that you lose friends or wound others' feelings?
- making a fool of yourself trying to impress someone?
- planning some elaborate excuse for getting out of something, only to have it backfire?
- using common sense to figure out a solution to a problem that has stumped others?
- trying to become someone you're not?
- honesty being the best policy?
- the mistake of being greedy? or selfish? or stubborn?
- figuring you knew more than you really do?
- how being older doesn't necessarily amount to being wiser?

You have the idea. Pick at least one of these generalized possibilities and write the story that it suggests to you. It should be true, not just true-to-life. Because our way of expressing our understanding of the rights and wrongs and the basic truths about life is usually through storytelling, you're already more a practiced and skillful storyteller than you think. All you need to get you started with the writing is a beginning you already know by heart: "Let me tell you what can happen when you...."

*　　*　　*

Stories can become as much a part of family possessions as scrapbooks and photo albums. Some stories trickle down from generation to generation. We never tire of hearing them, not only because they're amusing, but also because they form part of the glue that holds us together as families and helps us to know or remember the people who figure in them. Although you can't write up all of them, you can and should write up some of them, ones that you find particularly interesting or amusing. Such stories don't have to make a point, provide a lesson (although most stories end up doing this in one way or another). They don't even have to look like "stories"; that is, like the tales offered in this chapter and in literature texts, with a climax and a dramatic ending. Most family stories aren't so much "stories" as incidents—the time Uncle Fred drove the family Buick through the back of the garage; or when your grandfather let a skunk into the house because he mistook it in the dark for the cat. All families own good stories. But not all families are fortunate enough to have them in written form. Writing up family stories has launched some writers into a lifetime project. This may happen to you.

The Smithsonian Institution in Washington D.C. attaches enough importance to the idea of collecting family stories that they have sponsored a Family Folklore Project to encourage it. Their booklet *Family Folklore** offers very useful tips for folklorists, and if you decide to stick with this project, you

---

*Family Folklore, Interviewing Guide and Questionnaire. Folklife Programs, Smithsonian Institution, Washington, D.C. 20560.

should get a copy. One of their basic suggestions is that family members be interviewed, not just chatted with. A cassette recorder is recommended. They also point out that family gatherings provide ideal settings and along with this that group interviews provide natural ways for one story to lead to another or for more than one version of the same story to come out. The basics of good interviewing are spelled out too—questions that don't lead to *yes-no* responses; encouraging comments and an obvious show of interest in the person and the stories; the use of "props" such as photos, scrapbooks, and letters; and enough sense to stop pressing when someone simply doesn't want to discuss something or is tired or busy.

The Smithsonian booklet offers a sample questionnaire, although its writers point out that your own interests and the makeup of your family should determine what you ask. Their questions deal with some interesting topics, some of which might not occur to you. They won't necessarily come out in story form, but they're still worth writing up. For example, where did the family name come from? What does it mean? Are there any traditional first names or nicknames in your family? Do you have any notorious ancestor(s)? How did various relatives meet, marry? Have specific incidents in history played an important role in your family's history? A war? The Depression? Does your family have favorite expressions, sayings? How does your family celebrate holidays? Does it have any holidays that it has created and made a tradition of? How about traditional foods, recipes? Is there a family burial plot? What are the family's most treasured heirlooms? Who has the responsibility, official or otherwise, for being family historian? These questions are enough to get you started. Add your own. And heed this pamphlet's advice: Not all family folklore lasts long enough to move from one generation to the next. So, "Keep your eyes, ears, and mind open.... Collecting family folklore is one case in which too much is better than too little."

Write up just two family stories, the kind that you feel will be appreciated at home but that will also delight others beyond family members. Bring them to class to be shared. Be sure to offer them to your family too. (Get into the habit of sharing much of your writing with family members. Too often we overlook the readers closest to us.) Start an "album" of these writings. Discuss the possible value of such a collection, not only now but in the future. Consider seriously becoming the family folklorist. Certainly someone should. Why not you?

Moral: *You might as well fall flat on your face as lean over too far backward.*

I don't like the idea of starting with a point I want to make. I like better noticing how something takes on a high-lighted quality.

9

Just Stuff

i

Each of us probably has a few nuggets of knowledge buried away somewhere, astonishing bits of information that the rest of us either don't know or are misinformed about. Here's a brief list to get you started. Add your own to these, sharing in brief written form at least 2 or 3 little-known facts to enrich your friends and associates. Be choosy; make sure that your information is as accurate and well-researched as my facts:

1. Approximately 70% of tadpoles *do not* want to change into frogs.
2. In Scotland it's against the law to drive a plaid car.
3. J. Tugwell Crisp, not Charles Lindbergh, was the first man to fly across the *Atlantic*, a small hotel in Rutherford, New Jersey. Crisp made the flight without an airplane and was never seen again.
4. There is no North Pole. (There are, however, two South Poles.)
5. The mud-coated vireo was America's first national bird. By 1796, however, bald eagles had eaten them all.
6. In Finland one can be arrested for referring to a reindeer by his or her first name.
7. Circus showman P.T. Barnum's real name was Jumbo. (His star elephant Jumbo's real name was P.T. Barnum.)

Your turn:

8.
9.
10.

Not only are facts like these fascinating in themselves; often, so are the stories behind them. Please fill your readers in on the events surrounding one or more of the ten nuggets of knowledge above, yours or mine. (For example, what led up to Crisp's courageous but little-known flight? How are tadpoles polled?) Better to go with one of your own, though; you're the expert.

ii

I never buy things that require my assembling them. Mail order ads for attractive items that say in small print "shipped unassembled" scare me away, as do labels on cartons that claim "Easy to assemble" or "Goes together in minutes." The reason is that most manufacturers don't bother to write clear instructions. "Attach orange wire to ground terminal" isn't useful if nowhere do the directions say which is the ground terminal. "Place ends of Y-shaped brackets in appropriate slots in base" doesn't help much when there are two sizes of brackets, both shaped like Y's, or when there are more slots than brackets to insert them in. Such writing says only one thing quite clearly: "Now that you've bought it, it's your problem, not ours."

For those who sense that your future will involve instruction writing (and in various ways, nearly everyone's will), test your ability by providing a fail-safe, step-by-step set of instructions for those countless Americans who don't know how to give their 18-foot python a bath. You're encouraged to provide useful sketches to accompany the written directions. (This isn't quite as odd as it sounds. The best directions I've ever read were in a little book written by a veterinarian on methods for restraining various animals so that they could be safely handled and treated. He forgot to include pythons, however, so there's an important gap in the literature.)

The most useful, easy-to-follow instructions should win their authors something, I would think—perhaps a night free from homework. If the snake instructions put you off, deal with something that doesn't—how to serve in tennis, play stick ball, install a storm window, cook lasagna, etc.

iii

Here are five things that need unriddling. The first actually contains a complete message. See if you can figure out what it is. Once you do, cook up a few similar puzzles on your own to try out on family and friends. The second is a droodle, a puzzling arrangement of lines that, once explained, makes a silly kind of sense. You're invited to create a droodle or two, of course. The third and fourth are cartooned puns—plays on words, in these cases dealing with advice all of us have heard. This kind of word play isn't beyond you, either, nor does it demand great artistic skill. The last is I don't know exactly what, but it should bring out the playful foolishness that lies not far below the surface in all of us. I've provided an "answer" of sorts, but it isn't meant to be "right" so much as silly. See if you can top me. (Answers on p. 158.)

1. Sepcutember

2.

3.

4.

5.

Daring, dashing Dexter Bott could do
Amazing stunts, but not
Fly upside down without
(You fill in the last line.)

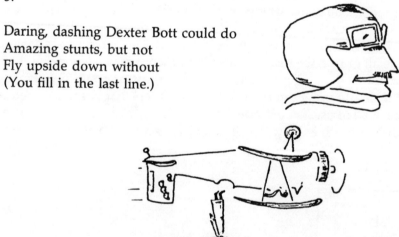

10

Stargazing

We re-make nature by the act of discovery.

Jacob Bronowski

This is a fairly accurate sketch of a group of stars that are easiest to see from about December through May. Not all the stars in the group look equally bright or large.

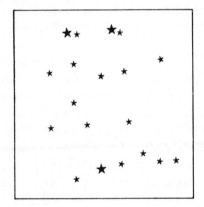

The stars form the constellation Gemini. They represent two figures from mythology, Castor and Pollux. Another name for this constellation is The Twins. The group of stars below seem brightest and easiest to see from August through October. They form the constellation Capricorn, or The Goat.

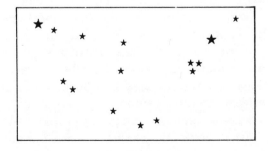

Do you see in the first sketch a set of twins? In the second a goat? Do you see any patterns at all, or do the sketches seem only to be a scattering of dots?

We have always been stargazers. Men and women have puzzled over the lights in the heavens since our time on earth began. Many thousands of years ago people began to read shapes into the stars and planets. The shapes were of objects they knew on earth—the dipper, for one—and figures from mythology, such as the Gemini twins, Castor and Pollux. Depending on the time of year and how clear the night sky is, we can see about thirty of these figures without using a telescope or even binoculars.

Really, though, the shapes aren't there. That is, they exist for us only after someone has pointed them out. Otherwise, you can stare at the stars night after night, month after month, and see only unconnected bright dots. Furthermore, it's possible to make many other shapes from the same star groupings. It's not like working through one of those puzzles where the dots are numbered and by connecting them we end up with a picture that was there all the time, built in by the puzzle's designer.

How is it, then, that ancient peoples, with nothing to guide them, were able to find and agree on these figures? Was it that thousands of years ago people had more imagination? Is it that we have outgrown the need to make connections between our lives on earth and imaginary symbols in the heavens? Could it be that finding shapes that really aren't there is as silly and superstitious as telling fortunes by finding patterns in tea leaves at the bottom of a cup?

The night's mysteries are not outworn, nor have our attempts to solve them ever been silly. Today, despite huge advances in scientific knowledge, the riddle remains: Is there a central scheme to the universe, and if so, how do we figure in it? The word *chaos* comes to us from the Greek language. We use it to describe extreme confusion and disorder. We talk about "chaotic traffic conditions" or the unordered chaos that exists in our minds when we puzzle over a tough exam or personal problem. To the Greeks, *chaos* was a label for the shapelessness of the universe. To make sense of chaos has been our concern from earliest times. It could be said that The Goat, The Twins, the Big Dipper—all of the constellations we have inherited from our ancestors—were ways of making sense of chaos, that the familiar designs are arguments against the seeming disorder of the universe.

The designs in the stars are projections of men and women's imaginations. They come from *within* us and not from any patterns that lived in the sky waiting to be discovered. When we write, we are seeking order too, answers not to the puzzles presented by the stars and the vastness of the universe, but to the countless things that live in our minds in loose, unshaped ways—to the private kind of chaos each of us seems to need to shape into sense. Can you see that writing is a way, perhaps a very important way, of making sense—that when we project our imaginations into words and sentences on paper we have forced some small part of chaos into an order? And that once that order is created, it can be connected to other ordered expressions, other constellations that you have shaped at other times?

What's a dipper?

Stop here long enough to write your responses to this experience and particularly to the paragraph above. Don't just answer the questions; it will be much more useful to use them as take-off points for finding how you really feel about this function of writing as it applies to you. Think all the way back to your first recollections of yourself as a writer, rather than dealing only in present terms. When has writing seemed an important way to work out puzzling matters? What kinds of writing, yours or others', is most obviously aimed at finding order? Can a poem be as much a way of seeking sense as an article by a scientist about the origin of the universe? What about a journal? free writing? a long, angry (or loving) letter, whether or not it gets mailed? a 3-page essay on the subject of "My Neighborhood"?

Look over the star patterns on page 53. Then copy or trace them as accurately as possible on a separate sheet of paper. Try to find the twins and the goat by sketching in lines that connect the stars. Be satisfied with simple stick figures. The completed constellations are on page 158, but don't check unless nothing at all forms for you after a half-hour of trying different combinations of lines to link the dots. (Two hints: the twins' heads are represented by the large stars at the top of the diagram, and the goat is facing left.)

*   *   *

Create you own constellation. Draw a dot pattern in which you can see a simple, recognizable stick figure. Don't use more than twenty dots. Trace a copy of your original dot pattern. Fill in the figure on one but not on the other. The one without the finished figure goes to a friend to work out. Be sure to name the figure too. And don't be tricky; keep the design figurable.

When you get your constellation back, perhaps you'll discover that another pattern has emerged from your friend. What do you make of that? Is he or she wrong? On a one-to-one basis, and then perhaps for sharing with a larger group, discuss the discoveries about seeing, thinking, and writing that this experience may suggest. It will be quite useful too to write up what you have learned about forming, both from your own working out of Gemini and Capricorn and the constellation your friend traced with you. Try to make connections that you sense may be important to your understanding of yourself and your private chaos.

11

Shopping Lists

Writing has awakened me. It makes me feel good. When I write thoughts down it helps me to understand.

Lisa Cole

If the riddle of the universe was a bit heavy to deal with, perhaps you'll find this closer-to-home riddle easier to handle: *How are supermarkets like shopping lists?* Divide a sheet of paper into two columns, one headed "Supermarkets," the other "Shopping Lists." Free up your mind, the way a runner loosens and stretches before a race. (Unlike the runner, though, be prepared to dash off in *any* direction. Don't worry about staying on the track.)

Now, without attempting to form any answers beforehand—to make any thought-out connections between supermarkets and shopping lists—jot down under each heading whatever comes to mind. Try to keep the jottings short, a single word, phrase, or at most a very short sentence for each entry. You aren't writing an essay about either subject, just listing ideas that surface in no particular order. Don't puzzle over your ideas; just get down rapidly and randomly your two lists. Give it 10-15 minutes, then quit.

What happened? Are you surprised at some of the things you jotted? At the length of either or both lists? Stop for a few minutes and discuss with others what you think happened *inside* you in the process of getting your ideas *outside*. It would also be a good idea to take a few quick notes about this for your folder while impressions are still fresh, sketching roughly what your mind was up to for those few minutes—how the lists got there, where they came from; how you sorted, selected, rejected, phrased; how you dealt with two totally unlikely topics in what probably were sensible ways. Can you find a pattern in the way you responded? Maybe, for example, you circled, as this writer did:

Shopping lists

paper
made from trees
trees in woods
wood for pencils
pencils make lists

57

Or made a leap from literal to figurative:

Supermarkets

Aisles like a maze puzzle
dead ends, confusion
mice trained in mazes
shoppers like mice

Neither of these approaches is weird. Both writers have made useful discoveries, not just about supermarkets, but about the way their minds track, and also about how writing can provide a map of sorts to show how ideas get from inside to outside.

As you look over your lists you probably see few likenesses and many differences. Fine. That was supposed to be the result. These two sample lists reveal nothing much in common either:

Shopping lists	*Supermarkets*
scribbled...backs of envelopes	high prices
always forget something	grumpy cashiers
No soda	babies in shopping carts
cross-outs	pyramids of cans
boring	fish smell...Yuk
Etc.	Etc.

Find a pair of entries, one from each list, that seem to have no connection whatever. Combine them into a single sentence. This isn't nearly as difficult as it sounds. Here are two to get you started:

The young mother scribbled a list on the back of an envelope while her baby screamed and kicked in the shopping cart.

Dad always seems to forget something when he goes to the supermarket, especially the soda and the high prices.

Try another pair, then another. It shouldn't matter which item from one list you match with an item from the other. (Don't bother with the one or two that, despite your best efforts, simply won't come together.) Move words and phrases around; rework the connections; tinker. Don't quit until you're satisfied with the way you've caught the surprise or sadness or silliness that lurks somewhere in any of these possible connections.

Now do the same thing with your own lists. Be fussy about the results; don't settle for absurd lines that result from quick and thoughtless splicing of items. If you bother to look for them, you'll find strong meanings, images, awaiting you in these scribbled-down fragments, and discovering them should be somewhat satisfying.

At least three good understandings should have come out of this experience: First, you answered the riddle. Shopping lists *are* like supermarkets. How? In exactly the way you've proved them to be—by finding seemingly different things about each that, to your surprise, came together into perfectly reasonable sentences. (You could have discovered the same thing, of course, by dealing with such unlike subjects as yo-yos and hand grenades or grass seed and zippers.) Second, you uncovered part of the answer to a much more important riddle: *What happens when I write?* Both novice writers and professionals face riddles every time they write. Always we work at making connections, often among unlike subjects. Nearly any magazine will reveal the truth of this. Look at the articles. They frequently deal with matters as different-sounding as shopping lists and supermarkets. What draws us to reading them is the very fact that the subjects *do* seem at first so unconnected: child abuse and alcohol, oil reserves and the threat of war, movie stars and drug abuse, hair styles and personality, etc. We as readers become deeply interested in the possible connections between unlikely subjects. Whether or not you plan to write magazine articles, this is a good thing to keep in mind.

A third understanding that could have come out of this experience is that it's entirely possible to produce a sentence or two this way that will push you to do something with it. Maybe the sample line about the woman in the aisle scribbling away while her baby howled and kicked could lead to something more, a fuller sketch of a confused and frustrated shopper caught in a typically painful situation. Such a line could be a way into a short story, poem, essay—or it could go nowhere. Once it's on paper, though, you have a chance to determine this for yourself. Look over what you've produced. Try to find a line that may be worth expanding. Expand. Revise, rework as you create. Perhaps in the finished version the original sentence will end up in the middle or at the top or bottom, or it may disappear altogether. It's not unusual for a writer to destroy the line that got him or her started. As for the rest of the sentences, put them in your folder, not in the wastebasket. That way you'll never have to say, "I haven't got anything to write about."

*   *   *

That the "Stargazing"and "Shopping Lists" chapters are arranged back to back isn't an accident. In dealing with the "riddle" that opened the chapter, it may have occurred to you that you were shaping a constellation of sorts too—seeking connections between elements that under ordinary circumstances aren't connected. Basically, you faced the same challenge as did our ancestors (who had neither supermarkets nor need for shopping lists): making sense, reducing a part of the confusion (chaos) of life, finding a solution of sorts to a mystery. Maybe it has also occurred to you that the supermarket-shopping list experience is a model that can be adapted to fit countless other confusions, large and small.

We're often expected to make sense out of chaos, to find connections between unlike or fuzzily related subjects. In school, it may be a request that we analyze something like Westward Expansion and the Slavery Issue, or make intelligent connections between Conservation of Natural Resources and the Energy Crisis. More personal and puzzling might be the struggle to fit together the relationships between your career goals and where and how to prepare for them. Like most people, too, you're probably faced with problems that seem to be made up of elements so opposite that they can't be brought into line—your sister's insistence on playing her stereo when you're trying to concentrate on homework; the need to catch the bus and your brother's dawdling in the bathroom every morning. How might the supermarket-shopping list model be applied to any or all of these matters?

Jot down three or four riddle-like subjects. Then find in them the most clearly opposing elements and reduce them to headings, giving them names (which isn't always easy). It might boil down to something like *Resources* vs. *Energy Crisis,* or *Charlie in the bathroom* vs. *7:30 schoolbus.* Apply the same approach you used in the preceding pages. Follow the process all the way through; that is, don't quit until you have in front of you the fleshed-out result of at least one sentence that you've created from elements of the two (or maybe even three) lists. There's a better than 50-50 chance that what you find will be revealing and useful to you. Like free writing, and any number of other writing experiences you're introduced to in this book, this approach should become one of your basic writing resources, something to be used again and again. Don't leave it behind you. A good way to understand the usefulness of such a resource would be to discuss at this point others' experiences in the working out on paper of these kinds of everyday riddles. If you think this process has worked for you, share your writing with others.

12

The Lamb Chop and the Wolf

There are a lot of other things besides nouns.

Gertrude Stein

We seldom notice in our own speech and writing how much we deal in what's-it-like kinds of language. The immediately preceding chapters have suggested that making connections among unlike subjects is something we must learn to do—that unless we think about it, practice it, it won't happen; that it's a special skill we must acquire to make us better writers. The truth is that it's a very natural tendency and that we do it constantly, not occasionally. We're always, it seems, making constellations, seeking ways to find new meanings or strengthen familiar ones.

One of my favorite lines is about old-time baseball pitcher Lefty Grove. It goes, "He could throw a lambchop past a wolf." What it means, of course, is that Lefty Grove had a terrific fastball. But when it's put that way, the ball doesn't seem to travel as fast. Both versions *inform*, but only one asks that we engage our imagination—that we create our own conclusions about the speed of Grove's fastball by picturing, perhaps, a wolf in a baseball uniform standing at home plate watching a lambchop go blazing by.

This kind of language is called "figurative," a label loosely applied to imagined associations between things rather than real ones: *she talked like a machine-gun; he's as graceful as a bulldozer; I was sweating bullets; my brother's a jackass,* etc. The other loose label is "literal," a term applied to "real" or "factual" reports: *it's raining; my big toe hurts; next week I'm going to St. Louis,* etc. The trouble with these labels is that they often lead people to believe that there really are two separate kinds of language, each meant to perform separate jobs—that literal language is, among other things, reliable, truthful, businesslike, and meant to carry information; and that figurative language is what we're supposed to use for poetry, exaggeration, love notes and amusement—to dress up or add "color" to speech or writing.

This is misleading. For one thing, distinctions are often hard to make. *My brother's a jackass* is obviously a figurative statement, but what about *My brother sounds just like a jackass when he laughs?* It could be literally true. For another thing, it doesn't matter at all whether or not you're being "figurative" or "literal" (if it's ever possible to be entirely one or the other); what matters is being understood, believed. Writers who strain to be "colorful" often sound fake; and those who work at being narrowly literal just as often sound terribly dull. The Lefty Grove line works simply because it says something *well*.

A college student came to me recently with a writing problem. He was working on a piece about building a log cabin. I had read an early version of the work and thought it was pretty good. His complaint was that it read like a set of instructions. "The problem is," he said, "I've written myself out of it. I've done all the stuff in here, performed all the steps, and I know how it *felt*, how much I loved doing it. But that doesn't show. When I talked about building the foundation, for instance—fitting one stone to another so you know they'll hold against the frost and the weight of the building—that's quite a feeling. I haven't said so. How can I do it?"

"By saying what it's like," I answered. "By comparing it with something that seems to have nothing to do with laying up a wall."

"I've been going crazy trying to find something," he said. "Once I got thinking about working with stone I knew the satisfaction of it wouldn't show if I just talked about how it's done, about the way to fit stones together. I even wrote a few lines of poetry about it, but I figured they didn't fit in a paper like this."

"They'll fit," I said, "if they say what you want to say. Show me the lines." Here they are:

> For every stone there is somewhere on this
> Rough land the stone that would be married to it.
> I am clergyman. I say the heavy vows.
> I wed stone to stone and know my wall
> Will last beyond a promise *I* may someday make.

Marrying stone to stone, performing a wedding. That's a good way to put it. It wouldn't be as useful to a wall builder as a simple set of instructions, but as a way to express this young man's sense of accomplishment, his satisfaction in performing a lasting act, it would be hard to beat.

Consider for a moment how you feel about this writer—what you sense you know about him, what kind of person he may be. Try to base your judgment on the lines alone, not what I've reported of our conversation. Discuss with others your sense about him. Then jot down a brief list of similar experiences and accomplishments of your own that might find strong expression through a comparison with another, quite different experience or accomplishment which would be familiar to many readers. The object is *not* to force you to write "figuratively"—perhaps to manufacture a connection you don't believe in, create an exaggerated or silly or flowery statement. With a list of subjects in front of you to consider, you'll find that one or two will suggest quite naturally some what's-it-like connections. Neither the subject nor the imagined connection need be terribly dramatic. It could start from something as simple as putting stones together the right way or teaching a dog to sit on command. The wall builder was looking for a way to make his reader know how he felt about something, not just how that something was accomplished. Do the same. What do you know that gives you special satisfaction?

- splitting wood? building a fire?
- drawing, painting, sculpting?
- writing a poem? a story?
- calming a cranky child?
- baking bread?
- sinking a basket?

Find a way to convey to yourself and others what the experience means to you. A short poem is one way, but there are others. Take your time. Don't quit until you're satisfied that the reader will know how you feel about the experience even if he or she has never enjoyed it or even done it.

13

Weeds, Seeds and Bones

> We can make meaning because we see in terms of what we have seen.
>
> *Ann Berthoff*

This is a picture of a gerzog. Write a 300-word essay about it.

Why haven't you started? Probably because you think you don't know any-thing about gerzogs. In a way, you're right. Unless I've picked the wrong object, you've never seen one of these things before. (If you know what it is, keep it to yourself, please.) Yet that's not really the same as knowing nothing about it. Maybe you don't know 300 words worth yet, but you know something.

When we're born we don't know much of anything. As we grow and learn language, we're gradually able to make sense of the world (although we don't all make the same kind or amount of it). At an early age you began to *conceptualize*, to move from a narrow recognition and labeling of particular objects, such as the wooden chair in your nursery, to an understanding of the nature of chairs in general, to the "chairness" of certain elements in your world. This process involves huge leaps of understanding. Humans don't plod through life making one-to-one connections among similar objects. That is, we don't have to work our way through chairs of all sizes and shapes to arrive finally at *chairness,* then go back and do the same for door to door-ness. Instead, we quickly arrive at a basic understanding of what chairs and doors are, no matter what size and shape they may be. Although you probably didn't know the difference between a Cadillac and a Toyota when you were three, you did know that they're both cars; and that a baby carriage, which also has four wheels and carries passengers, isn't. It didn't take someone's carefully explaining the differences between the two types of vehicle; the chances are that you figured it out for yourself.

Concepts like "chairness" and "carness" (and countless others) lodge in our memories and provide "frames of reference"—stored-away forms we use to test new things against the things we know. They provide us with the means for deciding that a gerzog is more like a *this* than a *that*. Language, along with the incredible reasoning power of the human brain, helps us make such connections. We're readily able to evaluate the similarities and differences between, say, a rock and a bowling ball, even if we've never seen a bowling ball before or even heard it named. Stored in our minds are concepts like *roundness, roughness, size, weight, ballness* (as opposed to *rockness*). With these we can arrive at useful conclusions. A chimpanzee can't do this; it would just as soon bowl with a rock. But even if chimps had a higher degree of intelligence, they couldn't learn as fast or as much as we do unless they also had a complex language such as ours and a brain built to use it.

Language is central to our ability to link stored forms. Saying is a way of *seeing, interpreting, knowing*. Even without these other objects in front of us, we're able to say that a bowling ball is somewhat like a grapefruit in shape, like a glove because both have finger-size holes, like a knife handle in that both are made of strong, dense plastic, even like an anvil, because both would cause pain if dropped on a toe. Without language, such conceptualizing would be impossible.

Past a point early in our development, we see almost nothing for the first time. Instead we *re-see*, bringing to the new object or situation all that's similar to it. One obvious example of this is the label we long ago gave to UFO's (unidentified flying objects): "flying saucers." Although these supposed craft were "unidentified," those who saw them (or thought they did) connected them with a well-known object, the saucer. Thus, in a way, they *were* identified, linked to an object we're all familiar with. Making connections between the known and the unfamiliar is a matter of re-seeing. It's impossible to imagine anything that isn't somehow like something else, something we already know. Without language, we'd have no free-flowing device for establishing likenesses and differences, for shaping the forms of knowing, for feeling comfortably curious about new objects and experiences, rather than hopelessly confused or even terrified by their strangeness.

Below is an article about an exciting find. Read it carefully.

WASHINGTON, Nov. 16—Anthropologists reported today that the largest group of complete skeletons surviving from ancient Roman times had been unearthed at Herculaneum, a town buried in the volcanic eruption that destroyed Pompeii.

The scientists said the discovery of more than 80 human skeletons was providing new insights into the searing, suffocating and nearly instantaneous death suffered by the citizens of the small Mediterranean resort in the eruption of Mount Vesuvius 1,900 years ago.

The finding of the first four skeletons in the group was announced two years ago, and additional discoveries have been made since then. But it was not until today that the dimensions of the find were reported.

Giuseppe Magi, the Italian director of the excavation, said the discovery revealed "a masterpiece of pathos."

The unusual collection of human remains is expected to yield a rich lode of scientific information about the life and health of the average citizen of ancient Rome. The bones hold a record that can disclose to scientists what people ate, their physical activity, their occupations and the diseases that afflicted them. Scientists say the more skeletons that are found, the more certainty with which they can make generalizations about society at the time.

Sara C. Bisel, a physical anthropologist who has been preserving the bones in a race against the ravages of time, told a news conference here that the skeletons were "a very major find" because of their number and their well-preserved condition.

In 1980, workers digging drainage trenches at an archeological site stumbled onto the first of the new batch of skeletons, which immediately caused a revision of historical views of the last days of Herculaneum.

Further digging uncovered more than 80 skeletons, 36 of which have been taken out and preserved. Italian archeologists suspect that hundreds more may lie nearby under a mountain of mud and hardened volcanic material.

The immediate message conveyed by the bones is the tragic human drama played out on the beach as people tried to flee. In one find, a dozen people who sought refuge under a seaside stone terrace appear to be huddled in embraces of protection and agony.

In another, a man with a sword still by his right side appears to have been slammed face down on the beach. And a sailor lies clutching an oar near the hull of a boat that appears to have been flipped upside down onto the beach....

When Vesuvius exploded on Aug. 24 [A.D. 79], it sent a column of ash and pumice 12 miles into the sky, where winds carried it to the southeast, gradually burying Pompeii but causing less immediate damage to Herculaneum. The next day, the vast column collapsed and sent a cascade of ash, pumice and hot gases roaring down upon Herculaneum, much like a snow avalanche except very, very hot.

It probably took less than five minutes for the surge to asphyxiate or burn its victims or smash them with debris....

Fortunately for archeologists, the skeletons were preserved in mud that was kept wet by underground water from nearby rivers. Once exposed to the air, however, the bones dry and crumble, so Dr. Bisel has been working since this summer to preserve them by washing, drying, and dipping them in an acrylic-resin solution to harden them for study.

She hopes eventually to have a population of at least 75 adult skeletons, the minimum she feels necessary to generalize about the inhabitants.

Thus far she has studied 26 adults. Based on this "very small group," she has found the average man was about 5 feet 7 inches tall, the average woman 5 feet 1½ inches. They were "rather healthy and pretty well-nourished," she said, with better teeth than modern-day Americans or ancient Greeks, perhaps because of a diet low in sugar. There is little sign of serious disease beyond minor arthritis....

The study of the bone structure of the skeleton found next to its sword suggests that the man was 37 years old, 5 feet 8½ inches tall, with arm bones enlarged by carrying a shield and throwing a javelin, knee bones adapted to accommodate the leg muscles of a horseman, and generally healthy teeth except that some appear to have been knocked out violently.

"He was a pretty tough character, a pretty impressive macho type of guy," Dr. Bisel said. But, with a long nose and missing teeth, "he really wasn't very good looking."

Notice that the accidental discovery of skeletons in 1980 caused a "revision" of what people understood about Herculaneum's last days. The bones told a story quite different from the old story. Furthermore, scientists working at the site expect to find many more skeletons. Is it possible that still new finds will again "revise" the story? Compare the use of the word *revision* as it's applied in this article with how you understand the term as it applies to writing. Jot down a definition of "revision" as you use it, and a definition based on how it's being used here. Discuss the differences.

Discuss these matters too: How is it possible for the scattered skeletons of eighty people to be read as "a masterpiece of pathos"? (If you don't know what *pathos* means, look it up.) How could one reasonably state, as Dr. Bisel did, that a 1900-year-old skeleton's owner had been "a pretty tough character, a pretty impressive macho type of guy"? From the brief description of bone structure, teeth, and probable muscular development, are other interpretations possible? What might they be? Why is it necessary to have "at least 75 adult skeletons" to "generalize about the inhabitants"? What will *generalizing* yield? Why wouldn't one or two skeletons be enough to form generalizations from? What generalizations have already been made? An anthropologist connected with the famous "Lucy" find in Ethiopia in 1974 commented, "Interpretation begins as soon as you find the fossil." How does this observation apply to the Herculaneum find? Just as important, how does it apply to bowling balls and gerzogs? With the idea of re-seeing? How is *revision* connected with re-seeing? Finally, what does any of this possibly have to do with writing?

Writing is a good way to find out how much we know (and don't know) about anything, whether it's a puzzling artifact like the gerzog (which is really a potato ricer) or a bit of fossilized human, or some shapeless problem that's bothering us. The Herculaneum scientists didn't write 300-word essays either, at least not at first. But they did use writing from the start. Almost certainly it was in the form of "field notes," on-the-spot jottings. Field notes are for recording impressions before they get away—for capturing early connections, interpretations, possibilities, as well as information like date, location, soil conditions, and other observable details relating to the find. Field notes are not for making final, ironbound conclusions. They're meant to keep thinking open, not shut it down too soon, so that it can be *revised* in the light of further discoveries.

Much early writing is guessing. Nearly all the writing you've done so far in response to this book has amounted at the start to guesswork. "Field notes" will provide another way to guess—to find out what you may know. You won't have to go to an archeological site to use them, either. You don't have to confront an object for the first time to discover it. What follows may sound dull or silly to you at first but should be just the opposite if you approach it with an open mind. No mystery objects and no skeletons. Instead, bring in with you some small, more or less familiar natural object, a weed or seed or shell or bone, and trade it without any comment for someone else's object. Whatever you end up with, take home. You're going to live with it for at least a week and write about it every day. Use the field note form described below, or one close to it that you devise for yourself. Don't be tempted, though, to use no guiding form. This field note format should work for you.

Rule off some sheets of full-size note paper into two columns the long way. Put the label "Field Notes" at the top. Over the lefthand column place the subheading "Information," and over the righthand column "Interpretations, Possibilities, Questions." The first column is for recording the more or less factual specifics that most people would note in one way or the other about your item. The other column is for your responses and questions; it's here that your observations are bound to swing away from what others would note. While you needn't become greatly worried about making distinctions between the two kinds of observations, try to determine which responses go where—which responses probably wouldn't come from someone else, as compared to those that we'd all agree about generally. It might help you to decide if you picture yourself an anthropologist or archeologist looking for the first time at an unearthed skeleton, first jotting down a fact—soil composition, depth of find, position of bones, etc.; then in the next column making some guesses—"looks at first glance like a child"; "could have been running"; "larger skeleton nearby also in running pose, so could have been parent and child," etc. Try to see one column as being "closed-ended," the other "open." That is, there's only so much "information" to record, but the other column could expand indefinitely. Here's a brief sample of what I mean.

Field Notes

Information (about feather)

Interpretations, Possibilities, Questions

5/11: Appearance—flat, spine-like thing (quill?) running down middle. Quill tapers to fine end toward feather tip. Actual "feather" part grows out of it evenly on both sides. On the other end the quill extends beyond the feathering.

Could be from seagull. It's gray and from a big bird (or small bird with one huge feather). Can't figure whether it's a wing or tail feather.

Measurements: Overall the feather's 10 inches long. The feather part is 8½ inches. The widest part of the feathering = 1½ inches.

Funny feeling when I run it through my fingers—and the light makes ripples in it, like water without sunshine.

The color is shades of gray with some whitish areas.

(sketch)

If I hold it up to the light, it's *solid* looking. No light gets through it. I never thought about a feather's being opaque (in fact, I never thought about a feather being anything much).

5/12: If I'm going to weigh this thing I'll have to take it to school. Too light to weigh on our scale.

Reminds me of a leaf—a fern leaf. Plants' feathers—Birds' leaves.... Poem here somewhere—wind blowing feathers backward, light undersides, like leaves turned up in a storm...?

I looked up "gull" in the encyclopedia. There are lots of different gulls, but most of them are gray. This is almost certainly from a gull.

I also am ready to say it's a wing feather. Noticed pigeon this a.m. (Also a big bird.) Wing feathers are more pointed at end than tail feathers. My feather's pointed too.

I wonder why gulls are gray and white. Is it for camouflage? Some birds blend with their settings, some don't (like parakeets, goldfinches). Is a gull this color so it won't be seen—so it can attack? Maybe to a fish a gull looks like sky through water.

5/13: Just figured that if a seagull weighs 2-3 lbs. and has maybe 10 feathers like this per wing—and I weigh 130 lbs, my feathers would have to be over 30 ft. long to get me off the ground!

I remember in a book I had some pictures of crazy contraptions people tried to fly with centuries back. Most of them were copies of bird wings. None of them worked. Now we have hang gliders, which are kind of bird-like in a way.

Encyclopedia said that water birds have glands to oil their feathers. I soaked this one in water and it got soggy. Probably it's dried up; the oil's gone.

5/14: This thing's closer to a knife- or spearblade than an airplane wing. And it does "cut" the air. So the design makes sense.

Looked up feather in dictionary. Not much help. It came from the Greek originally—3 words = *to fly, to fall,* and *wing.*

Sharpened the tip to make a pen out of it. It's hollow. Can't try it out. No ink.

5/15: Mr. Davies in science told me every individual little piece of a feather is hollow. No wonder it's so light.

Etc.

I never thought of birds being strong either, but pound for pound they must be much stronger than people. (Ants are. Somehow it's easier to think of an ant being stronger than I am than it is to think of a bird that way.)

It's hard to think of a "mistake" anywhere in nature. There's a reason for everything.

2 verbs out of 3. Can you use it as a verb? Birds "feather" their nests. You "feather" a canoe stroke. (I don't get the connection.)

Yes I do. My father also told me about "feather bedding." Putting more workers on a job than you need. Padding. Feather = padding (or maybe making the job as comfy as lying down on a feather bed).

There's a pigeon wing drooping from the gutter next door. It's sad-looking. I've never seen anything look deader.

Etc.

Actually, we use a "field note" approach whenever we confront something new or look at something more closely, whether it's a natural object, an artifact, a topic in school, a problem, or nearly any stray notion that happens to strike us. But when the "notes" exist only in our minds, they don't work nearly as well. A device like this one is extremely useful as a way to find out what and how much we know, as well as what remains to be learned. Writing it out this way (or in some similar form of your own) should, like free writing, become a writer's basic resource.

Before you go off with your weed or seed or feather, discuss how and why field-noting is proof that writing is more than a printout of thought; how "guessing" can be a more useful, powerful way into writing than outlining; whether this technique offers any new insights about what *revision* means, and whether possibly *re-seeing* might be a better name for this aspect of writing. Also, consider what writer Flannery O'Connor probably meant when she said, "I write because I don't know what I think until I read what I say." Finally, jot down a brief list of school-related subjects *other than English* where field-noting might be a very useful technique for learning (and although I said "other than English," consider too how it might help you deal with a difficult poem).

By the end of the week, begin generating some writing about your natural object. It needn't be a 300-word essay, although you should be able to see how even 300 words probably wouldn't be enough. Maybe you'll be moved toward poetry, or a song lyric, or a piece explaining how you felt about the week's experience. No matter what writings develop from this experience, you should plan on sharing them with your writing group and perhaps a wider audience after that. Readers may not be overly interested in a feather, but they'll be keenly interested in how *you* saw it.

*   *   *

While you're living with your object, here are three less-extended experiences that should add to your understanding of what writing is and does and how it can work for you. There are 21 items in each of the two lists below. Group the items in each list into categories containing 7 items each. Provide a title for each category. (Don't be too formal. "Seven Items I'd Hate to Step On Barefoot in the Dark" is a perfectly reasonable category.) Then in just a few lines explain (a) why you grouped the items as you did, (b) what you can now do with them—how, in other words, the grouping has helped you know something you didn't know before and (c) how writing helped you arrive at your categories. Also be prepared to explain (but not necessarily in writing) why your groupings are different from other people's. (You're allowed to use reference books, but don't start off with one.)

osprey
tree swallow
chicken
duck
Canada goose
turkey buzzard
partridge (or grouse)
seagull
robin
thrush
cormorant
canary
purple marten
redwing blackbird
turkey
pheasant
ostrich
quail
condor
golden eagle
peregrine falcon

tunafish
yogurt
ketchup
bananas
chicken liver
lamb
beefsteak
vinegar
tabasco sauce
spinach
sour cream
apricots
pizza
manicotti
bread
saltine crackers
flounder
salt
broccoli
ice cream
dandelion greens

Copy or trace the figures below. Place each figure on a separate sheet of paper.

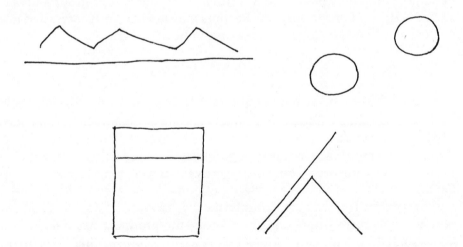

Write down the first thing the figure brings to mind. Then add a few sketched lines of your own, to make what you see in it clearer and more your own. (If in sketching, some other possibility emerges, go with it; you're not being fickle; you're only discovering something you didn't see before.) Explain more fully in writing what the figure is, now that you've added detail. Also jot down what other possibilities remain. Here are a couple of examples, both based on the first figure:

This is a clam's eye view of a sunbather asleep on a beach. It could also be someone waiting to be operated on, or a murder victim or someone braced against a wall (nobody said you couldn't stand the figure on end), etc.

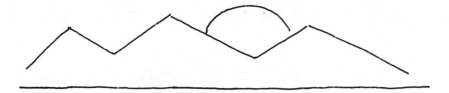

This is the sun coming up over the mountains. It could also be the sun going down, or the sun either coming up or going down behind a section of fencing; or the top of a lightbulb showing over a lampshade or part of a person's profile with an egg in his mouth, etc.

Now choose the most appealing possibility and add the details that only writing can provide: Where's the sunbather's wife? Has he fallen asleep and let his four-year-old wander away? Will his wife come back with three ice cream cones and be angry and horrified to find the child gone? Has he sneaked off from work for the day, and will his sunburn make a liar out of him tomorrow? Etc.

*   *   *

A number of households have at least one gerzog in a drawer or on a shelf or up in the attic—an artifact no longer used or recognized today but saved because someone in the family is a collector of old things. Bring it in and ask your group to see how much they know about it by means of a field note approach. In a way they'll be playing a game something like Twenty Questions, and although they may not in fifteen or twenty minutes get all the way to an answer, they and you may be surprised at how much gets discovered about your whatever-it-is.

14

Thawing Out

Alfred, the alligator is sick.
Alfred the alligator is sick.
W. Nelson Francis

Mechanics are people who work under cars. Here are pictures of two:

Mechanic: Someone who works under a car.

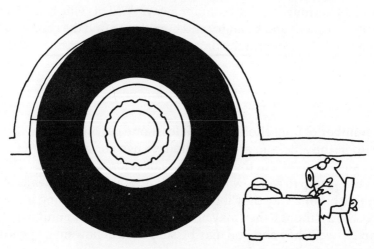

Mechanics is also a label for a part of writing, the part that has to do with capitals and apostrophes and other forms of punctuation.

Automobiles and writers both need mechanics. For the writer they're a code that readers need to get the reading exactly right. Put an apostrophe on the wrong side of an *s*, for example, and you'll throw the reader off; or stick a comma where he expects a period and you'll upset him, especially if you keep on doing it. In other words, jumble the code and nothing good can come of it. Someone may have taught you that mechanics are more important than the message—that what you have to say doesn't matter very much so long as it's punctuated properly. That isn't true at all; much terribly dull, empty writing is mechanically perfect.

Many grammar books take a similar approach, suggesting that if you march through miles of boring exercises, you'll "master" the apostrophe or conquer the comma. Such exercises make enemies of these little black things, as do papers that come back from a teacher marked with red ink meant to show you that leaving out an apostrophe or using a comma when a period was required is not only wrong but also earns punishment. The result is that many writers with perfectly good things to say develop a dread of punctuation, and the dread grows until the writer starts to freeze.

When a piece of punctuation no bigger than a flyspeck becomes a demon that leaves blood-red tracks all over your work, running from writing, hating it, is understandable. I wish there were an easy solution to whatever punctuation problems you may suffer—a simple rule to memorize, a model to follow. But many punctuation rules are puzzling; they seem to work much better in textbooks than they do when we try to fit them to our own words. "A statement is followed by a period" seems simple enough, but what a *statement* is is often unclear. The rule "Use a comma to set off nonessential clauses" works just fine in situations where what's "nonessential" is obvious, but quite often it isn't obvious at all. The sample sentences in grammar books are set up, most of them, to make the rule clear; they're usually not the kinds of sentences anybody writes. It does little good to study a sentence that goes "My Aunt Jennifer, who lives in Alabama, has a dog named Louise," unless sentences shaped identically crop up frequently in your writing. Copying and mimicking such model sentence structures can get you through exams, but it doesn't accomplish much else.

The best way to become comfortable about punctuation is to believe you have something worthwhile to say on paper. What should happen as a result is that (1) you'll write more often and more thoughtfully; and (2) you'll want every aspect of it to be right, including apostrophes. Meanwhile, don't let punctuation get to you. Consider that if you put together all the punctuation marks in our language, the list would be so short that you could hide them under a band-aid. Look:

BAND-AID   *PUNCTUATION MARKS*

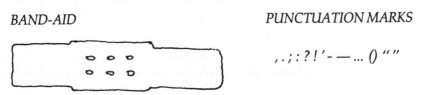

,.;:?!'- — ... () " "

Furthermore, no one has trouble with *all* of them. Usually it's only one or two that drive a writer crazy—quite often the apostrophe or the comma-period confusion. What do you have trouble with? None of them? Fine. Skip the rest of this section. Maybe, though, it will prove useful, so don't skip yet.

Some punctuation marks have weird names. Consider *parentheses,* for example. Strictly for amusement, your own and others', work these names into sentences that twist or change their meanings. Some of your lines may lead to a cartoon or two. Here are examples:

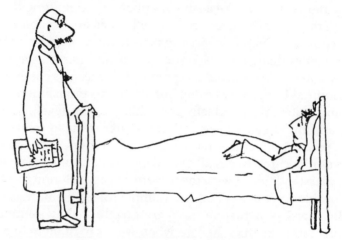

Sorry to tell you this, Sotheby-Jones,
but your hyphen's going to have to come out.

How about a sentence like *My father's moustache is as scratchy as apostrophes.* Or, *The chipmunk's cheeks bulged as if he had them stuffed with parentheses.* Or, *The breeze made commas on the surface of the pond.*

Creating a string of these dealing with every punctuation mark won't take long. Share what you come up with. Read them aloud to classmates.

Something about punctuation marks—their shape, what they do, how they look—suggests that they have a life of their own beyond being symbols written on a page. Play with this idea, either seriously or in fun. Here are three examples of what I mean, just to get you started.

A semicolon's	Something blew	I think that I
Momma is probably	Into my eye	Shall never see
A comma.	Last night.	A generous apos-
It's the father	What it was	Trophe.
That's the	I couldn't think,	*(Think about this one.)*
Bother.	Until I looked	
Is it	And found I'd lost	
Dash, or	The period at	
Dot,	The end of	
Or wot?	Inc	

Again, this is read-aloud material. It would be a shame not to share your punctuation play with others and to enjoy theirs in return. Whether you wrote a verse about being slashed by a dangerous dash, an essay about how to raise and train an apostrophe, or a song about the day it rained parentheses, what you've done is proof of at least three things: that you're capable of creating something fresh and different, no matter what the subject is; that your writing is amusing and interesting to others; and that mechanics don't have to be frustrating or deadly dull.

*　　*　　*

Most writers know writing mostly as a silent experience. The blank paper makes no sound, nor does your pen moving left to right across it, each letter hushed and obedient. So quiet is the writing that sounds you seldom notice become loud—the ticking of the classroom clock, another writer squirming in his chair. And then you turn your paper in, and it becomes part of a silent stack. In a couple of days—or weeks—it comes back, just as quietly, with a grade at the top and probably a written comment and some corrections. The whole process is so silent it's almost spooky.

The problem with all this silence is that you seldom *hear* what you've written. Because we've grown accustomed to writing as a noiseless process, we tend to close our ears to it and only *see* the words. Furthermore, we're frequently instructed to use only the sense of sight in writing: "Try and *spot* your errors"; "Can you *see* where you've left a comma out?" "*Look* over your papers before you hand them in."

Donald Murray, a writer and teacher of writing, says "The central act of writing is listening." I agree. And although he wasn't referring simply to settling punctuation questions by listening, your ear may be quicker and more reliable than your eye to pick up errors and guide you in making punctuation decisions that will have an effect on writing's primary aim—making meaning. Try *hearing* the differences between these two sentence beginnings: *I'm trying to tell you, guys,... I'm trying to tell you guys....* The pair of commas in the first makes its intention different from the second. Take a look at the completed sentences: *I'm trying to tell you, guys, I've missed my train.* Compare this with *I'm trying to tell you guys I've missed my train.* Which makes the difference stand out more, hearing it or seeing it?

If you engage your ear and not just your eye, you should be able to hear in the first one the *tell* rise just a bit more, as does *guys*. There's also a split-second pause after *you* and *guys*. The second version is flatter. The important difference between the two versions, however, is that they don't convey quite the same meaning, and writers must learn to care about even the slightest differences in meaning that such punctuation decisions can cause.

Question marks are easy to overlook, if *looking over* is all you're doing. For example, *What time is it* may not look as much like a question as does *Who are you*. But you can *hear* the fainter questioning tone of the first one, even if it doesn't jump out at you when you only *see* the line. On the other hand, *I wonder what time it is* looks like a question but isn't. The difference is quite easy to hear, even though the eye may be fooled. Inexperienced writers frequently stick a question mark at the end of a sentence like this simply because they haven't listened to it sounding like a statement, not a question. Exclamation points can also mislead when only seen. This sentence looks okay: *Rats, I missed the train!* But maybe it should be *Rats! I missed the train.* The first way the whole line shouts, as if the speaker is having hysterics. The second way it's only an angry yelp—*Rats!*—and then the reason behind it. Does it matter? When such choices have a bearing on meaning, it matters. Can you *hear* the difference in meaning between the two? Consider for a moment the differing reactions of readers to the two versions, which differ to the eye only in the placement of the exclamation point.

What does and doesn't go between quotation marks drives some writers batty. I've seen thousands of sentences from young writers that contain this kind of error: *She told him "she never wanted to see him again as long as she lived."* You don't have to read a chapter on quotation marks to avoid such a mistake. Just listen and you'll note immediately that *she never wanted to see him again as long as she lived* isn't what *she* said; it's what the writer put into his own words. What *she* said was, "I never want to see you again as long as I live." When you listen, the lack of her voice, her own words, leaps out. It should read, of course, *She told him, "I never want to see you again as long as I live."* Either that or, if you don't want your readers to have to listen to her yammering, *She told him she never wanted to see him again as long as she lived.* The choice is up to you, the writer. But if you hadn't bothered to hear the line, you might not even have been aware of a possible choice.

Do you see anything wrong with this sentence? *Setting your new quartz watch is easy, however, you should read these instructions carefully.* Maybe your eye caught it—the comma after *easy*. But buried in the middle of a page, the goof might slip by; your eye might miss it. You can *hear* the sentence ending on *easy*, though, and the way it mumbles and lurches uncertainly around *however* if you don't end it there. These are two sentences masquerading as one. The disguise may have tricked your eye, but it shouldn't have gotten by your ear. This is an example of the king cobra of punctuation problems—the run-on sentence.

Here's another example: *Frambling is a pleeked dollum, framblers never snerve before fremming.* Six of the ten words in this construction are pure nonsense; you've never seen or heard them before. Yet listening to it once or twice should have been enough to tell you that it's two sentences and that the first one ends after *dollum.* We're much more used to hearing our language than seeing it. From infancy we begin to learn the rhythms of English—to sort out by ear its shapes, its pauses, its stresses, rises and falls. *Frambling is a pleeked dollum* is a sentence, regardless of its non-meaning. You readily sensed it as one because you've heard the same rhythm countless times. *Framblers never snerve...* is the beginning of another. Your ear told you that the comma doesn't belong, that there's a full stop between *dollum* and *framblers.* It, too, has a strongly familiar set of sounds that, long before you understood the idea of *sentence,* took on a distinctly hearable form.

Listening can eliminate another construction that masquerades as a sentence—the fragment. *As we strolled under the towering elms* isn't a sentence, nor is *When Uncle George fell into the well.* Maybe why they're not sentences is perfectly clear to you at first glance. A good grammarian would be quick to label both of them "dependent clauses," and to quote the rule that "A dependent clause does not express a complete thought and cannot stand by itself." If you're like me, however, you don't have the faintest idea what a "complete thought" is, or in this instance why Uncle George's falling into the well isn't one. (What could be much completer than falling into a well?) I can, though, *hear* that a period isn't right at the end of either of these constructions—that something's wrong and/or missing. Probably you can hear that same thing. Make it *As we strolled under the towering elms, a faint rain began to fall,* and we can go along with it. (You can get Uncle George out of the well or leave him there. In either case, finish the sentence in some way that will get rid of the fragment.)

A nasty little mechanical problem that has nothing to do with punctuation but *does* have to do with hearing confuses some writers all their lives: the difference between *to* and *too:* You can memorize rules and hack your way through thickets of exercises, or you can begin listening for the differences between the two. Nearly all the time *to* sounds like *tuh* or *tah.* Few people say *I'm going tooooo the movies,* unless they're trying to impress someone. It's *...tuh the movies. Too* sounds the way it looks: *Alfie's going too.* Hear the difference?

You don't need exercises to determine what is and what isn't a sentence. You may need, however, to reawaken the life-long and very natural desire to listen for the ripples and hitches and stresses of language, this time as they flow from your pen.

15

Reading Is Hearing

I may consider a thing forty-nine times; but if you consider it, it will be considered fifty times.

George Bernard Shaw

Novelist Samuel Butler once wrote, "I always intend to read...what I write aloud to someone; any one almost will do, but he should not be so clever that I am afraid of him." So far, the idea of hearing your writing has had the narrow aim of helping you make decisions about punctuation. Furthermore, this kind of hearing has involved only the inner ear, the voice you hear when you listen to your writing within the privacy of your own head. Samuel Butler is talking about the out loud kind, where another set of ears comes into play. According to him, silent reading isn't enough, for he goes on to say, "I feel weak places when I read aloud where I thought, as long as I read to myself only, that the passage was all right."

What other kinds of "weak places" besides punctuation goofs might lie buried in the silences of a piece of writing? And how might reading aloud to someone make such weaknesses clear? Reading your writing to others can change the way it sounds to you, giving you still another way to understand it. Reading aloud also provides a way for you to get useful feedback from fellow writers. (Unlike Samuel Butler, you needn't worry about exposing your writing to someone too "clever"—a listener who is out to make you feel foolish. I think we've eliminated any such possibility by now.) This kind of experience can help you develop a sense of audience—to begin to know that much of what you write (but not all) should be meant for ears other than yours alone; that your words are capable of touching, delighting, informing others. Passing in a paper and earning a grade, even if it's a good one, is no substitute for a listener-reader lighting up and saying, "That was terrific! It really made me think" (or laugh, or remember). These are the experiences a writer cherishes long after grades have faded from memory.

Reading aloud will bring out the rhythms (or lack of them) in your writing. The way a line *sounds* can be as important as what it says, whether or not the reader is reading aloud. As readers, we "hear" silently, and what we hear influences what we understand and also how we feel. Any writer should be aware of this. If you like the way something you've written sounds, there's a good chance that it also says what you want it to—that sound and sense are working together to produce the effect you want. This is tough to talk about but not to hear. Compare the two beginnings below. Both say approximately the same thing, but they're nevertheless quite different. Read both silently and aloud more than once.

One Sunday, in summer, a few years ago...

There was this one Sunday a few summers back...

Now quickly jot down two or three endings for each sentence. Don't labor over them; just let the lines push you in whatever directions they seem to dictate. Then read the different versions of each to your reading group. Discuss which of them *sounds* best in each case, and why. Also discuss why the first line led writers to shape somewhat different endings than the second line did. (Maybe this didn't happen, but it usually does.)

The first line was written by William Butler Yeats, probably this century's greatest poet. (Never mind who wrote the second one.) Yeats didn't use it in a poem, though. It's the beginning of a small memory piece about his native Ireland. The line is soft and warm-sounding. By creating small pauses, the commas hold you back. They lull the reader, suggesting a sense of the slowness of Sundays in summer. Beyond their actual meaning, which tells us the day, the season, and the general time ("a few years ago") is the rocking sound of the syllables. Listen:

Sun   sum   few years go....
One   day, in   mer, a   a

It's difficult for the reader to rush this rhythm. Try shifting the three phrases around. What happens? It doesn't have any effect on the literal meaning of the line, but does it have any effect on how you react to the information?

The second line also tells us the day, the season, and the time. But its sound is very different. The lines use five words in common (*one, Sunday, a few, summers*), and they both have the same number of syllables. How would you label the differences (faster, slower, louder, softer, etc.?), and what do you think accounts for them? Yeats apparently wanted to slow us down. What might have been the other writer's intent? Here's what one writer developed from this line:

There was this one Sunday a few summers back, August sometime, and me and Uncle Gabe was sitting down by the lake. It was right in the middle of the day, and the sun was hot and high and bright. I'd taken off my shirt, but Gabe, he had on the same things he always had on—white shirt, overalls, crunched-up sailing cap, old heavy workboots, probably even an undershirt.

Discuss how your reaction to this might have been different had the piece started with "One Sunday, in summer, a few years ago..." Also discuss what hearing the differences out loud had to do with your reactions.

Try using one of the following sentences as a way into something longer. Use any of the sentences or change the words of any of them, but keep the general shape and rhythm of the original.

Take two old tire tubes, truck-size if you can find them.

Once I'm sure that it's not going to rain that night, the rest is easy.

Being patriotic does not mean simply putting up a flag on June 14 or the Fourth of July.

What should happen (although it won't always happen) is that as you fit words to shape (or vice versa), you'll also begin sensing an idea to go with it. Perhaps it will be only a glimmer at first: Let's see; something *did* happen *one weekend, in August, before we moved here.*

How does what you've written sound after some reworking, tightening, tuning? To find out, go off by yourself and read it to a dog or a tree or a mirror. Even better (much better), read it into a cassette player or tape recorder. This way you can become your own audience before going public. What sounds flat or sour? What lines, regardless of what they mean, simply don't fit together? Tinker some more. Then listen again. And again.

Now try it on another audience, your fellow writers. One sensible word of advice first, however, that applies to all writers. When you respond to another's writing, don't be "clever." You and the writers you work with share the hope that what each of you has written will reach and please another. Responses like "It stinks" or "What boring stuff" hurt, and accomplish nothing more. Finally, *listen.* Jot down others' comments in the margins. You're the musician playing the piece for the first time. If you hear and absorb, you'll play even better next time.

writing to be read aloud:

16

Indenting

Telling someone to practice writing will get you about the same results as telling a pullet to practice laying eggs.

Me

Riddle: What is almost always longer than a sentence but shorter than an essay? Answer: Lots of things. I was hoping, though, that you would say "a paragraph." Some writers have argued that this is all there is to know about paragraphs; that if you boil away all the complicated rules and definitions about them, it comes down to a writer's making personal choices about where and how often to divide writing into paragraph-size units. According to this thinking, there's no absolutely right or wrong way to construct a paragraph. Indeed, "paragraphing" may not be a separate writing skill at all; and, therefore, studying paragraph construction and doing exercises in "paragraph building" may be a waste of time.

Here's a paragraph about paragraphing I wrote in a letter to another teacher:

I remember a time in life when I became desperate to find the magic formula for concocting topic sentences. Begin each paragraph with a topic sentence, I had been led to believe, and all of life would become describable. I recall Miss Scudder, our fifth-grade teacher, putting up on the blackboard "Good penmanship is a sign of good character," and explaining why this was a topic sentence. I had no idea what she meant, but I passed most of my assignments by starting each paragraph with sentences modeled along the same lines: "Good apples is a sign of a good tree," which not only led me further from the truth but also took all the zip out of my prose. I know now that either every sentence is a topic sentence or none of them is, and I gave up caring years back.

The other side of the argument is that just as we must master the forms of the sentence, so too must we become thoroughly familiar with the packages in which they're put, paragraphs. And just as there are specific rules about sentence structure, so too are there rules to learn about paragraphing. The basic argument is that paragraphs should have a topic sentence, and in most cases it should be at the beginning, that a good paragraph (like a good book, toothache, or hippopotamus) should have a beginning, a middle, and an end, that it should, according to one composition text, "mark a stage in the writer's thought" (although these stages may vary in length and method of organization, they will contain a general statement [the topic sentence], which is supported by specific details), and that because good paragraphs should contain these necessary elements, they must be carefully planned in advance.

What's wrong with the first argument—that a paragraph is whatever the individual writer wants it to be—is that it provides absolutely no useful guidelines and suggests that paragraphing is as personal a matter as choosing one's brand of deodorant. What's wrong with the second point of view is what's wrong with many statements about writing: in setting up rules, the rule-makers don't allow for individual differences, matters of choice about purpose and style. Inexperienced writers, led to believe that paragraphs can be divided into two groups, good and bad ones, may end up writing sentences like my "Good apples is a sign of a good tree" because it seems safe, even if it also seems silly. Rules about writing are fine, as long as they're based on some knowledge about how writing actually works, instead of on decisions about how it *should* work. It isn't natural for a writer to fret about rule-breaking instead of getting words on paper. If you're the kind of writer who finds it helpful to first settle on a so-called topic sentence and then outline the details of a paragraph, fine; that's how you should go about it. If, however, this approach seems as unworkable as buttoning up your shirt before putting it on, just write; seek out your paragraphs later.

The paragraph you've just finished reading, by the way, has no topic sentence, or if it has, I don't know which one it is. Nevertheless, it holds together; nothing about it seems odd or wrong. The rule I broke goes, "A paragraph should have a topic sentence, which states the main idea." The truth is that many paragraphs do not have such a sentence—the kind that stands out from others in the paragraph like a St. Bernard in a pack of chihuahuas. *It's perfectly possible for a paragraph to have what passes for a central idea without its being caught in a single sentence.*

Here are some other generally accepted truths about paragraphs that it should be useful to know:

• *Paragraphs have no grammar of their own.* "The geese overhead on their way to nesting grounds far to the south" is not a sentence. It lacks a verb. When we try to read it as a sentence, we're bothered; something's wrong. A basic rule of grammar has been broken: *Sentences require verbs.* This is a grammatical rule; nobody passed it, anymore than anyone voted in favor of the law of gravity. It simply exists. English sentences, no matter what their length or subject, are controlled by a very specific set of such grammatical rules. But no such right-wrong laws govern what is and what isn't a paragraph.

• *Paragraphs, unlike sentences, exist only in writing.* Written sentences are coded reflections of speech. Because for the most part we speak in sentences, we nearly always write in them. We do not, however, speak in paragraphs. (We may seem to in formal situations such as prepared speeches and debates. These are usually based on *written* notes, however.) Thus, the paragraph is not a coded imitation of the spoken language, and we have no natural tendency to write in them, as we do to write in sentences.

- *The paragraph was originally devised to give the reader a rest.* Centuries before anyone determined that paragraphs should have topic sentences, Greek scribes placed this symbol (¶) in manuscript margins at various points. The mark was meant to signal resting places for the reader's eye, not to point out "stages of thought." Paragraphs continue to have this original function today. We are accustomed to the visual breaks provided by indenting; a page without such breaks suggests that the reading will be tiring and difficult, no matter what the subject. Thus, whether or not the paragraphing of a particular piece of writing really divides the subject into smaller, easier-to-understand units of meaning, we at least think it does.

- *Paragraphing does not determine whether a piece of writing is "good" or "bad."* Readers seldom judge a writer on the basis of how he or she structures paragraphs. Readers seldom, in fact, single out a writer's paragraphing for any kind of criticism at all. Most often we're not even conscious of it. The sentence, not the paragraph, is the living cell of writing. When we talk about a writer's style, we're referring to the way that writer uses language, not the way the paragraphs are arranged. If we like the writing, it's mostly because we enjoy the way a writer has shaped ideas into sentences and how they build into something that amuses or interests us. Our liking has almost nothing to do with paragraphing, or if it does, we're usually not aware of it. Writers come to know that the real struggle in writing is not to form model paragraphs but simply to make the next sentence as good as the last one and to have the two work smoothly together.

- *Paragraphs aren't writing.* The prefix *para-* means "beside," "alongside of," "beyond," "aside from." *Graph* (as the word is being used here) means "something written." These definitions together tell us that a paragraph is something other than writing—something outside or "beyond" the act of writing itself. Another way to put this is that while writing can (and sometimes does) exist without paragraphs, paragraphs cannot exist without writing. This may seem as obvious as saying that heads can exist without headaches, but headaches can't exist without heads. But it's meant to point you toward a slightly deeper truth: that paragraphs are only *forms*; they should not be mistaken for the *meaning* we may find in them. As a student you are probably often asked, "Write a paragraph describing...." We hear this instruction so frequently that it's easy to start believing that writing and paragraphing somehow amount to the same thing. They don't. Writing is the creative act of shaping thought into sentences, making meaning on paper. Paragraphing is much more mechanical. It amounts to deciding that certain sentences have enough in common to roost together in paragraph form. When you are asked, "Write a paragraph about...," the instructor probably means "Write briefly about...." They aren't the same thing.

• *Paragraphing can help writers to re-see (and therefore may be more useful to writers than to readers).* For many writers, paragraphing is at the very center of revising. Remember, revising is *re-seeing,* and a good way to see more closely what you've said is to find the beginning of an order and then move the writing around, adding and eliminating, until the order grows stronger and clearer. Until, in other words, the whole thing comes together into a beautiful kind of satisfying sense. The trouble is that writing doesn't always "move" that easily. When we face three or four pages of our own words, it can be tough to pick through the mass of it to find out what it really says and to go about making its meaning sharper. What has to be moved? What stays and what goes? Where's the beginning? What do I want it to look like?

Often, pulling together just one paragraph from the jumble can provide an answer to one or even all of these questions. Make one tight paragraph and you will have forced a piece of the final whole into being. This can make the next paragraph easier to form. Even if you paragraphed the first time through, this kind of re-seeing can be useful. First-draft paragraphing is often no more than indenting out of habit or because it looks neater. You're bound to see and hear things that didn't fall soundly into place the way you first put them down. Therefore, it's a mistake to think of these first-time-through paragraphs as rigid molds into which your words are locked. (Sometimes a piece of writing falls nicely into place as it comes out, but this is more luck than skill.)

Note: This "truth" is not a *rule.* The truth about writing is that there isn't any set order or system that works for everyone.

• *It's more important to know it's a good sentence than to know it's a topic sentence.* I'm not suggesting that topic sentences aren't useful. They can be, for both writer and reader. But too much fuss is made about them, especially in composition texts, and it has led to wrong notions. Many writers have done exercises where they're given what's supposed to be a topic sentence and told to provide a paragraph's worth of details to support it. Here are two such practice sentences, each from a popular textbook:

> *My recent trip to California was enjoyable in every respect.*
>
> *In every home certain jobs should be delegated to the children.*

What these sentences have in common is only their dullness. Yes, you can form paragraphs to support either of them, but who would want to? Furthermore, they are *not* necessarily topic sentences at all. The truth is that any sentence can be a topic sentence if that ends up being its function. It doesn't have to have the puffed-up quality these sentences have. And I worry that if you do enough of these kinds of exercises, you'll believe just the opposite: you'll begin thinking that unless you have a dull, fat sentence squatting at the top of every paragraph, you're wrong. Every sentence should be as tight and powerful as you can make it, whether or not it fits the textbook definition of *topic sentence* or *supporting detail*. If in your writing you can't find any sentences like the ones above, congratulations!

If any sentence can be a topic sentence, how can you know whether or not a paragraph has one? Most writers don't worry about this. What a paragraph is—where it begins, what it contains, how it ends—can be determined only by the person who forms it. We look at the sentences on a page, sense that meaning is somewhere in them, seek ways to organize that meaning, try to pull together a paragraph or two, then look again. Each time we do this it's for the first time; we have never formed such a paragraph before. If we like the way a paragraph hangs together—if it seems a smooth and useful piece of the whole—then it probably has in it a sentence that seems to pull other sentences together. But this doesn't mean that you must be able to label it "topic sentence." Giving a sentence a name doesn't make it any better or different.

When a group of sentences seems to belong together but lacks a center, it bothers the writer. If we can't find in there the line that we imagine we need, we cook one up. It's part of the urge to make our ideas clear to ourselves and others. It's also very pleasing. To watch a sentence that we create from nothing pull meaning from other sentences is a private delight that has nothing to do with following the rule that says paragraphs must have topic sentences to decorate their tops. For this reason it's seldom fun or profitable to write paragraphs around someone else's version of a topic sentence, whether it's about traveling to California or anything else.

• *We learn far more about what paragraphs are by forming them from our own sentences than by studying about them in books.* Therefore, the only sensible request to be made at this point is that you stop reading about them and write instead. About what? Anything. But if that suggestion is too vague, turn back to "Remembering." Go through the chapter again. Your life isn't just a matter of *now*; your past teems with things worth writing about.

17

More Stuff

i

A friend recently told me that in a survey of some kind, "cellar door" was felt by many people to be the prettiest sound in our language. What do you think? What about a word or phrase makes it attractive, aside from its meaning? Does its shape have anything to do with it? Or is it purely a matter of sound? Certainly, it isn't always meaning. There's nothing particularly pretty about cellar doors.

What are your candidates for prettiest-sounding (or -looking) words or phrases? See if you can come up with three or four that strike you as being extremely attractive to your ear and eye. Disregard meaning entirely. That is, don't list *chrysanthemum* because it happens to be your favorite flower. It's more interesting, for that matter, to list words whose meanings you may not even be sure about.

My favorite word is *nuance.* I like the silky flow of it. It looks attractive too, with no itchy-looking letters sticking up or dangling underneath. I like these words too: *anesthesia,* which sounds like a Greek goddess or a small, lovely country; *tamarack,* which is a softwood tree but seems to suggest by its sound and shape that it's a musical instrument or a town in New Jersey or a type of brittle candy. *Ambiguous* is kind of fun. It seems to gather itself into a ball, leap in the air, then come down and bounce away. And then there's *serendipity,* which to me sounds like the name of a fabric pioneer people used to sew long, flouncy dresses from, or a dance done to fiddle music, or a mild rash you can use for an excuse not to go to school.

Based only on the sound (and possibly the shape) of their names, what are your favorite countries? Never mind where they are or what their climates are like; we're not concerned with that. (I like *Estonia, Samoa* and *Patagonia,* which, I've just discovered, reveals a liking for two-vowel endings.) What are your favorite states or countries—places you've never been but that you're drawn to because the sound of their names is so attractive?

Jot down a random list of words that because of their sound and/or shape appeal to you. And give some reasons why, the way I did. With others in your group or class compile a *Word Lover's Dictionary* composed of terms you and others have come up with. Following a basic dictionary format, divide the master list among you and cook up your own definitions based on the first things a word's sound and shape remind you of. (Use of standard dictionaries is strictly forbidden.) Example: *oblivion:* 1. A type of aircraft that flies only in circles. 2. A military weapon used in the 14th century. 3. A native of the nation of Oblivia. Be sure to provide at least one sample sentence using the word in each defined way.

(Note: This experience will also provide interesting results using weird or ugly-sounding words, as well as terms from other languages. Many of us have friends and neighbors who speak a second language at home. While you may not understand quite why, a word or phrase from another language may strongly attract you.)

ii

Here's a poem by a young writer who decided to shape his poem to *look like* its subject.

                    My Uncle
                         Kenny
                              Used to
                              Buy me
                         Long,
                    Stringy li-
                    Corice
                         Whips—
                                   Ten cents a-
                                   Piece.
                    Black and red
                    Licorice
                         a
              Yard long. I
              Could eat li-
                    Corice all
                         Day and
                                   Not
                         Get sick.
                    I
              Used to
                    Mash it
                         Into
                    Marblesizeballs.
                              Alan M.

This writer used a similar approach.

> My body
> In a cor-
> Ner in a
> Box feels
> Pinched,
> Legs crack-
> Ing, Arms
> Bending,
> Squeezing
> And squir-
> Ming to get
> Every last
> Inch of fl-
> Esh in.
>
> *John H.*

How would your reactions to these writings have been different if you only heard but didn't see them? The unusual way these young poets tried to make words look like the subject instead of just explaining adds an amusing dimension to the reading. Here are three other examples of writing that play with the same idea. In these cases, the fun is almost entirely in the seeing.

1. Last weekend we got a flat tir
                              e.

2. What do you see when you trot? Not   aw   lot.
                                        an   ful

3. (I forgot to close the parentheses, and a
                                          l
                                          l

                                          t
                                          h
                                          e

                                          .

                                          .

                                          .

Your turn:

4.

5.

iii

A college student of mine is a collector of baseball cards. Recently he was offered two thousand dollars for one of his collection, an autographed 1958 Willie Mays card. Two thousand dollars! An advertisement for a New York City gallery recently offered the following for sale:

A two-page letter by S.L. Clemens to Robert Barr, a novelist. It was written in 1897 and contains some comments about Barr's writing. The price: $2500. (Who's S.L. Clemens, anyhow?) A 19-line letter written in 1863 by Abraham Lincoln to his Secretary of War requesting the release of a couple of young prisoners of war. The price: $3500. A two-page letter dated December 31, 1783 written by Thomas Jefferson to Benjamin Harrison and dealing with European politics. The price: $5500.

Do you think the prices placed on these letters would be less if each dealt with other matters—if, for instance, Clemens had written about the weather, Lincoln about a leak in the White House ceiling, Jefferson about the difficulty of getting reliable help? Suppose you had the chance to own one of them. Forgetting its dollar value, which one would you choose? What would you do with it? (No, you can't sell it.) A more complicated question: What personal value might it come to have for you? Why?

Here's a list of well-known people, some living, some not. Copy the list and using a scale of one to twenty, rate the value you would place on a letter written by each of them. (If you don't know who some of these people are, look them up.)

Barbara Walters	Greta Garbo
John Lennon	Charles Lindbergh
Emily Dickinson	Martha Washington
Al Capone	Babe Ruth
King Henry VIII	Neil Armstrong
Margaret Thatcher	Marilyn Monroe
George Armstrong Custer	Amelia Earhart
Muhammad Ali	Robert E. Lee
Howard Cosell	Florence Nightingale
William Shakespeare	your great-great grandmother

Discuss and defend your choices. Write a letter to one of your live top choices. There's a good chance you'll get an answer. If you do, don't try to sell it.

18

I'm Fine, How Are You?

...letters are certainly the honestest records of great minds that we can become acquainted with.

William Hazlitt

Novelist Ernest Hemingway once said, "I write letters because I love to get letters back." I can't think of a better reason. In my village, even a blizzard doesn't stop people from trudging to the post office in the morning. Like me, like nearly everybody, they can't wait to see what has come in the mail. There's something about an unopened letter that makes us anxious to get at what's inside, even if we're pretty sure it isn't good news. And yet how often have you heard the comment, "I hate to write letters." Or "Sorry, I just haven't had the time to write." Or "I *owe* Uncle Ben a letter" (as if you had borrowed one and needed to return it).

According to postal authorities, people don't write personal letters as often as they used to. Instead, we're becoming a nation of card senders. No longer does the greeting card serve only for such special occasions as birthdays and holidays; shops now offer all-purpose cards meant to be suitable for any time, any occasion. In addition to thank-you and sympathy cards, we can now find I-miss-you cards, I-love-you cards, even I-think-you're-a-jerk cards.

The greeting card business is a huge one. It has grown so partly in response to the slump in letter writing. It's quicker and easier, obviously, to shoot fifty cents worth of manufactured message at a friend than it is to spend a half-hour or so writing a letter. Probably, too, you can count on pleasing the person who receives it. Cards are pleasant reminders that someone out there has thought about us, if only long enough to sign and mail a card. But a card is no substitute for a letter. Card manufacturers print as many as 100,000 copies at a time of some numbers. When you pick one off the rack, consider that it's a duplicate and that enough copies may have been printed to be sent to every human being living in Cleveland County, Oklahoma. How personal can such a card's message be? Not very. A letter's better. Letters aren't manufactured; they're composed. They're not meant for an audience of 100,000, only *one*. It all comes down to this: if you care enough to send the very best, send a part of yourself; don't settle for a mass-produced version of who you are and what you want to say.

There are times, of course, when a card is entirely suitable. Sometimes a card's message says it exactly right. Sometimes you *are* in a rush. Sometimes a particularly pretty or funny card that we stumble upon brings someone to mind and awakens a slumbering friendship. Sometimes, too, for reasons each of us knows best, a personal letter just doesn't seem to fit the circumstances. This isn't meant, then, as an attack on the greeting card, just as an effort to save the personal letter from extinction and to bring it back to where it belongs: near the center of communication between people who care about one another.

I've just spent an hour trying to find a birthday card for my Donald.
They're all meant for children much nicer than he is.

Such one-to-one writing opportunities should be inviting. Not only is a personal letter *free* in the sense that they cost nothing; they also offer the writer more freedom than any other kind of writing meant to be read by another. No rules govern what you must and must not say, or how a letter must look, or how long or short it must be. If a business letter requires the kind of composition and design that suggests getting dressed up on paper, then a personal letter is by comparison barefoot, relaxed, even rambling.

And very, very private. We don't write such letters to submit them for a grade or to be shared with an audience any larger than the named audience on the envelope. (*Private* isn't meant to suggest *intimate* or *confidential*. Whether or not a letter contains comments that would make you blush if it fell into the wrong hands is not the point. *Private* here simply means one-to-one, not one-to-many.)

What's more, the personal letter offers what too much school writing doesn't: an authentic, engaged reader—someone who has nothing to do with classrooms and assignments; someone who is eager to read your writing. Someone, in other words, who feels just as delighted to hear from you as you are when you receive a letter. It becomes relatively easy to write a paper for school without aiming your words at anyone in particular. But try writing a letter that way. It simply won't work. There may be no better way to understand what the idea of *audience* is and why it's so crucial to all writers than to consider the difference between the picture of another person that comes sharply to mind as you write a letter and the vacuum that forms when you're told to write a composition on something like "Our favorite family holiday" or "Some chores bore me." (Many textbooks assign the practice writing of personal letters. In one I found this remarkable request: "Write a letter telling your parents that you have arrived safely at the Kicking Colt Dude Ranch in Kingman, Arizona." If I discovered a child of mine writing such a letter, I would send him to bed until he stopped hallucinating.)

With personal letters you don't have to wait for something newsworthy to happen. In fact, good letters often come out of those times when we feel a faint itch to write but have nothing specific in mind to say. In this respect, the personal letter is like most of the writing we've been talking about: it's a way of finding out what's on your mind. Because a letter is a way to close distance, it can be enough to let your reader see what you're seeing at the moment. That's how this long-ago letter to a friend began:

> Dear Frank,
>
> What I see before me now as the sun rises this morning are the narrow, gray-black road that runs westward into the valley and climbs eastward to Summit, the highest community in this county; a black rooster and three red hens that examine the porch floor for insects; a small, weathered barn whose insides overstuff it and spill in a jumble from doorway and loft; a steep hillside freshly scarred by a dozer and topped with white birches; an urn of pansies and dwarf marigolds; a red panel truck; and a scruffy brown dog.

It's likely that some small matter that amused you will amuse a friend too:

> Dear Bill,
>
> Just the other day I heard another funny story about Cyrus, our only local character. Cyrus used to have fits, although why and what kind no doctor ever figured out. They were only partly legitimate anyhow, according to Charlie. He said Cyrus would have a fit once or twice a

year, whenever it seemed like a good idea. Then he happened to let himself get stricken in front of two old ladies who live just down the road. Greatly concerned, they picked him up, carried him into the house, put him in bed and fed him. That ruined him, Charlie says. After that, Cyrus would have two or three fits a week, always in front of the ladies' house—sometimes right up on their front porch so they wouldn't have to drag him too far.

Here's part of a letter that got written because the writer wanted to share a *smell* with the reader. Although this seems an unlikely reason to write, it interested and pleased the person who received it.

Dear Annie,

My cabin has a clean, woody smell. Not the flat, dry smell of a lumber shed or the sour odor of heaped, fresh-cut pine logs, but the tangy, faintly sweet smell of drying sap. It's a fresh scent, stronger still in the loft than on the main floor. Up there the long, raw, half-rounded rafters angle downward from peak to deck at the room's far edges like the ribs of a capsized ship, and I can smell their light, drying aroma close over my bed.

It's a young cabin, set amidst century-old apple trees gnarled and bent away from the northwest wind that comes cruelly out of the flat mountain sky and down over the haylot's brow. There were farms here then, when these trees bore dark-red, tough-skinned fruit. *Arabia,* they called it, this isolated settlement whose haycrofts and cattlebarns have long since settled under a thousand snows, after the people and the cattle left and the roofs went cold and could not shed the weight of the snow. Only the laid-up shale foundations stay, the best among them still true enough to build on again, the flat, interlocked slabs holding against the grindings and heavings of deep frost.

Onto this twice-old land, ancient in name and again in abandonment, I came with trees fresh-dropped and drawn clean of shaggy, red-brown bark and sawn into sills, joists, studs and rafters, then heaved and hammered into place. It oozed and wept at first, every stick of it, the stove drawing the stored water out of the wood, the windowpanes wet with it every day, the frame members emitting startling explosions of drying at night, the whole of the process scenting the place so strongly that I could taste it in my food. Now, though, it has softened as the timbers have grown harder and drier, and when I enclose the inner walls with sheetrock, only a stranger to the place will note the smell.

Letters are a good place to let out memories and frustrations too. The letter below began on a note of irritation. Its writer went on for a couple of pages about his annoyance with the racket being produced by the family TV, wandered into a reflection about old television shows, and ended—

It wasn't all bad, of course. On Friday nights, particularly in summertime, the appliance store proprietor would often leave a television set running in the window. Friday nights were fight nights. People would drift up in the warm darkness and gather around the window. The group would swell to fifty or so if a good fight was on. We'd stand there touching shoulders, sometimes jostling for a good spot. We didn't mind the lack of sound. Two fighters were hitting each other, and we didn't need a shrill-voiced announcer to tell us who was getting the better of it. These summer nights are a good, warm memory for me and probably for others too—standing shoulder to shoulder in shirt-sleeves with strangers watching the Friday night fights coming from St. Nicholas Arena and not being afraid to talk.

Clearly, writing out the frustration helped. What began in annoyance ended in a pleasant, satisfying recollection. The reader benefited too. Earlier in the letter the writer's comments lost their angry note and became quite funny, and the conclusion above allowed the reader to share still another part of the writer, this one from deep in the past.

It could be argued that any letter to a friend is in a way a love letter, a way of saying "I'm thinking about you; you're often in my mind." The phrase *love letter*, though, suggests writing so terribly personal that it shouldn't be allowed in a book like this. Therefore, no examples of love letters are offered, save this one, written over forty years ago by a six-year-old boy to a pretty blonde girl who sat just one seat ahead of him in first grade:

You a big cat.

The girl wadded it up and threw it at him, which broke his heart. He had thought it the very finest of love letters—an offering of the only words he knew how to spell.

Some types of personal letters are expected of us; they're associated with politeness, good manners, being a responsible family member. The thank-you note is the most common example of this kind of letter. Have you ever been told something like "Go upstairs right now and write a thank-you letter to Aunt Louise"? Probably. Such politenesses are expected of us all, old and young alike. But when we write letters out of duty or because we've been forced to, they're usually awful. Such letters often begin and end in such emptinesses as—

Dear Aunt Louise,
Thank you for the wonderful bath powder. I used some last night and just love it. I'll use it next time I take a bath too. It has such a nice smell. I hope everything's okay with you and Uncle Fred. Thanks again.
                                                                Love,
                                                                Alice

That gets that over with. You've done what was expected. But consider that when an aunt or an uncle (or whoever) receives a letter like this, they recognize that it's only a gesture—a response as manufactured as a greeting card message. Alice wrote the note, but she's nowhere in it. Let this kind of hollowness come from someone else's pen, not yours. It's as simple a matter as not forgetting the *person* in *personal* and saying thanks as if you meant it deeply enough to offer a small part of yourself in gratitude.

Any of us could without much effort jot down a list of people we should write to. Audience is not a problem for the letter-writer. Time is not a problem, either, although we most often use it for an excuse. Nobody is too busy to write one or two letters a week, which is enough to get you firmly stuck in the letter-writing habit. Start this week. Make up a list and post it in plain sight by your desk. Consider it just long enough to determine (a) who would most delight in hearing from you; (b) who you have ignored so long that you've begun to feel twinges of guilt; (c) who you would most like to get a letter from; (d) who you may lose as a friend if you don't write; and (e) who on your list comes most clearly to mind; who can you most sharply picture sitting there reading your letter? Probably everyone on your list is going to fit one or more of these considerations. Keep in mind that long before you've written to all the people you listed, you'll start getting letters back and that, like Ernest Hemingway, you'll love it.

*　　*　　*

We've been over this before, Billy. Write to Santa and you know he'll get it. With the Tooth Fairy, it's strictly hit or miss.

If everybody wrote to at least one stranger, we'd cut way back on the misunderstanding and foolishness that separate people in this world. Others who feel this way have formed organizations around the idea. You can start a friendship with someone either here or from another country by writing to any of the agencies below. They'll send up-to-date lists of names and addresses of young people anxious to do the same thing. (Be sure to state your age when you write.)

Afro-Asian Center
P.O. Box 337
Saugerties, NY 12477

(Requests $.80 fee. This organization accepts requests only from "teachers and other responsible leaders.")

International Friendship League
22 Batterymarch Street
Boston, MA 02109

League of Friendship
P.O. Box 509
Mt. Vernon, OH 43050
(Requests $1 fee.)

Letters Abroad
209 East 56th Street
New York, NY 10022

Student Letter Exchange
910 Fourth Street, S.E.
Austin, TX 55912

World Pen Pals
1690 Como Avenue
St. Paul, MN 55108
(Requests $1 fee.)

Although not all agencies request it, enclose a stamped, self-addressed envelope. Young people's magazines and hobbyist publications sometimes include offers to send pen pal lists too. Teachers often have sources for pen pal names and so do librarians. Write to someone, anyone. If you do, one less person will trudge back empty-handed from the mailbox.

By now perhaps you've begun to believe that there are few better ways to get to know a person than through his or her writing. You can spread your circle of acquaintants and friends tenfold by collecting others' words on paper. As odd as it may sound, you can even get to know and like people who are no longer alive. Letters especially make their authors knowable. They're often the most natural kind of writing people engage in, the kind that lets the writer show through. Like old journals, letters from another time are also sometimes rich in history. Read the following letters a couple of times through; then discuss what you sense about the people who wrote them and the time they lived in. Consider how these letters are a blend of skill and no skill; and why (if you agree) this blend adds charm to the whole—and may let us know and sense more too.

Fremont, Colorado
August 28, 1892

Mr. A.P. Wood

Friend Amos,

You will be some what surprised to hear from me but that revolver you got me gave such good satisfaction that two of the boys want me to get one for them just like it. by the way it saved one fellows life. I loned it to a fellow by the name of Whitmore one day. He was prospecting and was panning some dirt in the crick and did not notice some cattle that were kept working up on him until a big bull snorted close behind him. there were no trees or any place to get. the only thing to do was to fight. He shot Mr. Bull twice. the second shot droped him dead in his tracks. Now Whitmore says he must have that gun or one just like it so if you will get me two and send them by Express I will pay you the money as soon as they come. I do not ask you to put them in at cost prices or any thing of that kind. You probely remember what it was but I will describe it again to make shure. Two 44 Smith & W. using the Winchester Cartridge 44s, six inch barel blued. Double action. Just send the bare guns and will send back the money by return mail. If you don't wish to do this send them C.O.D.

Hope this will find you all well. I am still working in the mines. I have not made any strikes on my own property yet. but there are about 15 shipping mines now and they keep striking them every little while. But things are very dull around town except Saturday night and Sunday. then there are rather lively times. Friday night there was a woman shot in a resterant. and one poisoned herself a few days before. There has been a number of deaths here that have been hastened either by a doce of lead or something of the kind. But they say that this is the quietest mining camp they ever saw for one its size.

Give my regards to all.

Headquarters 9th Army Corps
Near Burks Station
April 19 1865

Dear David:

This is the first opportunity I have had of writing to you since Adam was killed. We have been marching on the track of Lee's Army since the 3rd of April when we left our old camp before Petersburg and marched through the city. I would have enjoyed two or three hours in the city fine if Poor Adam had been alive but as it was I had no heart for anything. Cartloads of tobacco lay in the streets and no end of whiskey in the stores. I got alot of segars but that was all I cared to take. We had got about 57 miles of the other side of the City when news of Lee's surrender reached us. This brought us to a stop and here we lie still. I have been awful busy since we stopped working up all the orders etc. that were issued during the march. I would not have had the time to write to you today but there is no work allowed to be done on account of the death of the President who is to be buried today. You will have heard all about the capture of Petersburg just one week after Adam was killed. The canonading commenced on Saturday night the 1st April at 10 o'clock. at 12 at night all the batteries on our whole line were firing over 400 cannon were firing til about half-past 3 on Sunday morning when they stopped for an hour and a half when I fell asleep but it was not long that I slept for one gun in the centre opened at the end of the hour and half and in half a minute the whole Batteries were roaring louder and faster than ever. It was awfully grand to hear that mighty roar of artillery mingled with the shrieking and whissing of the bombshell as our gunners showered them into the Rebel lines. I lay in bed and listened to it, pitying the poor fellows who were in the midst of it and glad that poor Adam was where the roar of battle would never more disturb his rest. I got up at daylight and packed up ready to march and then began the most deadly part of the battle. Five brigades charged the Rebel works and the sickening roll of the volleys of musketry along with the cannon made the Battle Complete. A faint cheer now and then could be heard coming from between the lines as our men captured Fort after Fort. I wanted to see as well as hear so I crossed over the Railway bank and saw the Field of Battle covered with smoke. I could not distinguish the men but I could see the fire flashing along the line as the various regiments poured in their volleys. Then the long string of Ambulances reaching from the end of the smoke, coming slowly along their way to the Hospitals with the wounded. Sometimes a larger 4 horse wagon piled up with dead would come along. And going towards the fight 6 horse *caissons* going at full gallup with ammunition to the Artillery. Men going to the rear wounded in the hand or arm but able to walk. Pack mules carrying cartridge to the infantry. Cavalry Patrols galloping along reeping up stragglers and the gallant "19th" stretched out to pick up skulkers and puting them into the Guardhose. After we left Petersburg the whole line of the March was covered with clothes, letters, etc thrown away by our troops. The country this side of Petersburg is very fertile and beautiful. The fields are out of cultivation but the Peach and Apple trees are all in bloom and there is whole acres of Orchards along the roads. The Peaches will be ripe in July and if we are here we can have some fine feeds. However the War is over for us now when Lee has surrendered. Peace may not be declared for some time yet though, as Johnstone still has an army that has to be whipped before that event.

This is a manifold writer paper I have written to you on, what we write the dispatches on when we are in a hurry then we write 3 or 4 at a time. When I have done I will have three copies of this letter besides the one I send to you and everyone escactly the same as the other.

...Rember me to Agnes Clachrie and ask her why she don't write...

In your house there may be letters from relatives and friends of another time. In many attics and unopened drawers are people who still live in letters. Read them through. There's a very good chance that you'll enjoy the experience. If you can get permission, bring one or two to school to be shared with others. Consider too, of course, what your words on paper may

Courtesy of the Delaware County (NY) Historical Association.

someday mean and how important it becomes, when you think about it, to link ourselves in letters to people who may otherwise never get to know us.

*   *   *

Look back at the letter from the young Union soldier. It's on-the-spot reporting of a fierce battle, one of the last in the Civil War. But it isn't "history." We'd wonder at such writing in a history text or encyclopedia entry dealing with the Civil War. There's somebody right in the middle of this reporting—a youngster who lay awake in the dark listening to the "grand" sound of cannon and thinking not about winning the battle but about "the poor fellows" who were on the receiving end of the shelling; a soldier grief-stricken over the loss of a close friend, yet still curious enough to go out of his way to watch the fighting; a letter-writer so eager to let his reader share what he saw and felt that he jumped from describing the horror of wagons loaded with dead to a glowing description of the countryside without preparing the reader for the jolting shift of subject.

I think it's a remarkably good letter, powerful and moving, yet without any signs of being polished or labored over. How might this young man have responded on paper if he were sitting in a classroom after the war and was told to write a 500-word essay on the Siege of Petersburg? I'd bet that he'd make a hash of it, that his essay would be stiff and flat and downright dull; and that it would take him five times as long to write it as the letter took.

It's an odd thing. People who write strongly and fluently in a letter to a friend often choke when they're asked to deal with the very same subject in a different form—an essay, for example. Why do you think this happens? Wouldn't it seem to figure that if you can say it in a letter, you can say it someplace else just as exactly and convincingly? Yet I can bat out a pretty decent letter just about as fast as I can type, but it may take me all day to produce just 25 lines of manuscript on the same subject. Dozens of people have said the same thing about their own writing. Perhaps you're aware of it too.

Once a professor used a Greek word in a rather complicated lecture. The term threw me, and because the lecture's main point was built around the word, I came away confused. The dictionary didn't help much either. So I wrote a letter to a friend. In it I complained about the use of such hifalutin words and went on to detail my confusion. When I read the letter over, I found that in the course of writing it, I had defined the term and that the professor's main point had become as clear as a bell. No miracle had occurred. In the comfortable privacy of a personal letter I'd relaxed enough so that I could ramble into some meaning. Had the professor assigned an essay at the end of his lecture, I'd have flunked.

There are two messages here: the first is that we almost always know more than we think we do, and the second is that a letter may be the best form to use for finding out the truth of the first message. Why? Easy. A letter is *authentic;* it's written from someone to someone in an honest attempt to communicate. Ideally, this is what all writing is for, but we all know it doesn't work that way. As essay isn't necessarily written *to* (or even *from*) anyone. And many essays, particularly in school, aren't attempts to *communicate* but attempts to *pass*. Big difference. Another advantage to finding out by letter is that it's *tentative* and *private*. An essay is neither; it's not a place for fumbling around, guessing, wondering. And it certainly isn't private.

At least three passages in this book were originally parts of letters that I wrote to a friend when I got stuck trying to explain something. That should suggest to you still another useful writer's resource, one that will keep on working for you all your life. When you're stuck—when you can't find a way to deal with a question or problem, whether it's school-connected or personal—write a letter to a friend. Relax, take your shoes off, let whatever is on your mind come spilling out. If it's a physics problem or an issue in social studies or a gut-level, personal concern, you'll find a way to put it that will be natural and honest.

Of all the writing devices recommended in this book, this one is absolutely guaranteed. You'll find yourself writing faster, more confidently, less stiffly than in any other form. And once you've discovered through a letter that you know more than you thought you knew, you can move your discovery into other forms with confidence. Try it; it works.

19

Cookieology

Me wan' cookieee!
Cookie Monster

What do you do with a cookie? If you're like most people you push it into your face without a second's thought. The cookie may be the most un-thought-about product in America. Cookies are a staple in nearly every home. In any medium to large supermarket are upwards of a hundred brands of them, and annual sales figures in the *billions* of dollars. Cookies have even worked their way into the language as figures of speech. A moustache is often referred to as a "cookie duster." When we're nabbed snitching something, it's said that "We got caught with our hand in the cookie jar"; and if bad luck strikes we write it off as "the way the cookie crumbles." The cookie is also the ultimate symbol of gratitude and affection. Consider what we leave for Santa on Christmas Eve. It isn't pizza.

Yet in no serious way do we attempt to understand or honor the U.S. cookie. No school offers a course in it, and except for cookbooks no one writes about it. We have no National Cookie Day, nor has the Postal Service ever thought to put one on a stamp. Nowhere in our nation is there a state cookie, nor even a tiny village named after one.

You can do something about this. Why should you bother? What if Columbus hadn't bothered? We wouldn't have a Columbus in Ohio or a Columbus Day. What if Isaac Newton hadn't bothered? Can you imagine a world without gravity or fig newtons? Without your founding the field of cookieology, how can this wonderful product be understood for what it is, a vital national resource? As a cookieologist you'll be breaking new ground as well as correcting a national wrong. You'll also be learning something— about the cookie and about yourself as a writer about the cookie.

In nearly all research it's expected that the researcher won't let person-al feelings enter into the study. We wouldn't think it right for an ornitholo-gist, for example, to state in a piece of research that she thinks it boring to hide in the bushes spying on birds. But although facts will play a central part in your work, so will you. You can't reasonably be expected not to fall in love with your subject and to let your feelings leak into the language of your find-ings.

Facts first, however, and a language to put them in. This is a new science and lacks the specialized terms that research requires. You and other pioneers in the field shouldn't settle for such sloppy terms as "kind of gooey" or "crumby." A few useful terms already exist, labels such as *brittle, chewy, grainy, smooth, dark* and *light chocolate, chocolate-coated, creme-filled, fruit-centered, oatmeal, coconut-topped, sugar-* and *cinnamon-sprinkled; ridged, embossed, waffled; marshmallow, nut, butterscotch, lemon, ginger,* etc. From memory—or better, after browsing the cookie section of your supermarket—come up with additional terms. Be sure to include labels for shapes. Beyond wafer and sandwich cookie shapes, there are at least fifteen others. You'll find domes, manhole covers, and puffs, for example. Create your own terms and through discussion settle on the ones that seem best.

This will also help you and your colleagues determine what is and isn't a cookie. Lately, candy-like products have been sneaking into the cookie sections of supermarkets. Are they cookies or aren't they? Is a "hermit" a cookie or a small cake? How about the brownie? Is the familiar graham cracker a cracker or a cookie? What will you decide to do about the Chinese fortune cookie? The animal cracker? With a set of specific terms you can make sensible determinations. If a product doesn't fit your careful definition of *cookie*, exclude it, unless you're the kind of researcher who would just as soon let a partridge slip into a study of chickens. Keep in mind, though, that unless you have a reliable way of determining what your subject *is*, it will be difficult to separate it from the things that it *isn't*.

Except skimpily, no one researcher can take on all cookies. Often in basic research the temptation is in this direction; young people especially believe that the broader the subject, the easier it will be to write about. Not so. What's interesting and useful lies most often in the specifics within a broad field of study. This is as true for reader as writer, by the way. Would you rather read an article on professional football or one the same length about the last quarter of a dramatic play-off game? About mammals or the harp seal? About bakery products or the chocolate chip cookie?

If by this point you're even faintly interested in cookieology, you must choose a narrow course and plunge deep into its specifics, leaving your colleagues to do the same. Your contribution to the field could be in the area of economics—a study set up to determine the best buy within a category based on ingredients, weight, shelf life (how long the product will last before going stale), taste, consistency, and price. Or perhaps consumer analysis is more interesting to you—the age, sex, family and income status of buyers of two or three distinctly different types of cookie. Learning about and charting the sales cycle of cookies by type could be interesting too. When does a type of cookie tend to sell best? Least well? Do some cookies sell strongest in the morning, late afternoon, or evening? Weekdays or weekends? Summer or winter? Does shelf placement seem to have an effect on how a type of cookie sells? Is there a way to determine what packaging has to do with the way cookie consumers make choices? What about brand loyalty? Does the consumer of cookies within a category choose a certain brand because he or she always has? Does the family shopper buy the same types of cookie every week as a rule?

Where will you go to find information on any one of these topics (or another topic of your own invention)? What methods would you use? What possibly useful conclusions might such a study yield? Who should you be aiming your study at? Don't be too quick to answer these questions. Research has a way of yielding approximately as much fascination and value as the time and ingenuity you invest in structuring it.

*   *   *

As a fledgling cookieologist, you may find yourself drawn into an additional in-depth study of just one cookie, probably the one you're most deeply in love with. Here your purpose may be less to inform than to convince—to provide persuasive proof that your readers should feel about your subject as strongly as you do. Simply gushing on about the product will convince no one; argument must, to be effective, rest on evidence. Following are tests to which you should put your cookie. Each requires exact standards of measurement and an honest reporting of results. (How to arrange the tests is up to you.)

- The how-high-will-a-small-dog-jump-for-one test. (Be sure to note the dog's color.)
- The how-long/loudly-will-a-baby-cry-if-you-snatch-it-away test.
- The how-many-seconds-before-it-turns-to-glop milk-dunking test.
- The is-it-possible-to-stuff-a-whole-one-into-your-mouth test (an important concern in classrooms).
- The is-it-possible-to-play-a-harmonica-just-after-eating-one test.

(List two or three other equally useful tests that come to mind.)

The cookie interview should, of course, be a central part of this study. How (and please be fair with your responses) would the cookie of your choice be expected to answer the following questions?

1. What ingredient do you feel proudest of? most uncomfortable with? somewhat embarrassed about?
2. What famous monument or architectural style do you feel you most resemble?
3. What cookies do you feel superior to, and why?
4. Is there a cookie that you secretly envy?
5. What well-known quotation seems best to apply to you?
6. What celebrity is it easiest for you to identify yourself with?
7. What famous historical figure?
8. What's your favorite novel? song? movie?
9. How would you describe your mating call?
10. What's your middle name?
11. Does all that cellophane make you feel...well, naked? (or, Does being in the dark inside a bag or box depress you?)

12. Do you ever feel the urge to be alone?
13. What do you *really* think of the neighbors?
14. Who is your favorite consumer? Does being squeezed by shoppers bother you?
15. What's your favorite spectator sport?

(Add four or five more questions of your own devising.)

16.
17.
18.
19.
20.

(It would be amusing—and a fair test of your accuracy—to read these responses to classmates. Use a Twenty Questions format and see if they can identify your cookie.)

Other evidence-gathering methods are also available to you. Handing out samples and recording taster responses will provide opinions other than just your own. So will brief interviews of people who purchase your cookie. Their responses could provide what in advertising is called a "testimonial," a statement of high praise from somone who likes the product. To provide evidence of your subject's popularity, a few questions directed to the person in charge of the baked goods department might reveal that yours is one of the best-moving cookies in the store. If you also dealt with the earlier subject of price *vs.* quality and quantity, perhaps you can argue that your cookie is a great buy at the price. Or that it's especially nutritious, or low in harmful ingredients, or artificial preservatives, or calories. What other methods occur to you?

If you think that this has all been played strictly for laughs, you're quite wrong. Sure, the subject may be a light one, but whoever said that research had to be a sober, gloomy experience? So far, if you've put your heart as well as your sense of humor into it, you've involved yourself in the same kinds of defining, labeling, choice-making, field study, data gathering and analysis that confront any researcher, regardless of the subject. In fact, what you've experienced is much more typical of research than would be a week or two in the library taking notes on a subject that other researchers have already written up. Here, that's left to you; it's your findings, not another's, that now form the source materials for readers. And that is no small thing.

How you write up your findings is up to you; no formulas or models exist in this new field. If you write to *inform* and/or *persuade*—if you sense that what you have uncovered depends on *you* and not just "the facts"— what you finally arrive at on paper will be worth reading. Keeping yourself in your writing is the only way I know of to feel any deep responsibility for what comes out. Listing neat little facts isn't enough; computers can do that. But no machine has a point of view, or a sense of humor, or any desire to please and inform another.

In addition to swapping and discussing with colleagues these foundation stones of cookieology, these findings *must* be shared with as broad an audience as possible. Oral reports or a special issue of the literary magazine are two means. But you can draw support and attention to your crusading efforts in other ways too: Announce a National Cookie Day (or at least a National Cookie Break). Adopt an official school or community cookie. Design and get a handy classmate to make a flag. Write to the company that produces the chosen cookie and inform the president of your choice. (If you think you won't get a response, you're dead wrong.) Send a news release to local papers or radio stations announcing the founding of cookieology and your research to date. Be certain to bind in permanent form this first book in the history of the universe on cookieology.

(Afternote: Founding a new technology, in this case *cookieology,* can only happen once. With just minor changes, however, the process outlined here could just as well apply to such other sadly neglected products as umbrellas, bubblegum, snorkles, comic books, paper clips, yo-yos, or approximately eleven thousand other subjects that cry out for attention.)

20

Writing about Others: Live People vs. the Other Kind

Louis XIV became King of the Sun.... If he didn't like someone he sent them to the gallows to row for the rest of their lives.

A college student

For many years as an English teacher I gave out such assignments as "Pick a historical figure who interests you and do a brief paper on him or her," or "Here's a list of ten writers whose works we'll be studying. Choose one and do a short report." What always puzzled me was my students' lack of enthusiasm for such projects. And what often made me furious was that most of their papers came in stuffed with ideas copied nearly word for word from library resource books. It finally dawned on me that what this kind of assignment really asked was "Write freshly and originally about some famous dead person you don't know anything about." And that, of course, is impossible.

Writing about the famous dead can be a deadening experience, and it's hard to figure why students are so often asked to write about people who fall into this category. It isn't that there are no *live* people to write about. At this very moment more than three billion of us occupy this planet, and most of us are more interesting than the other kind. Almost none of us is famous, either, which means that you can pick nearly anybody for a subject without having to plough through encyclopedias and old magazines for information. An additional advantage to writing about one of us unknowns is that the choice is your own; it won't come from someone's list of approved subjects. This gives you the chance to be the expert; instead of producing one of those repeat-and-report papers based on others' writings, the contents of this work will be entirely your own, a matter of your discoverings and no one else's. Knowing that you have caught the shape and sound of another person on paper can be far more satisfying than rehashing dry facts about a dead one.

Anyone is interesting to write about. Inside each of us and mostly unknown to all but a few is a person remarkably different from all the rest and well worth writing about. And while no writer can hope to reveal another

*Not only will this have immediate benefit for all mankind;
it'll make us one heck of an essay topic for generations to come.*

person fully, you can offer glimpses that will make your subject knowable. Here are a few such glimpses, each from longer works.

Grandma's boots are wet with dew. So are her coveralls, soaked and darker blue to the knees. Her crimpled, dusty hat becomes her.

Todd R.

Uncle Charlie's short and plump. It always surprised me how fast he could move. For years he fooled me with the same corny trick. He'd have the ball one minute and it would be gone the next. He'd say "The ball's in your pocket." It always was.

Paula S.

Walking into the house I hear the happy, off-beat tune. It's welcoming. My grandmother is in the kitchen whistling to herself.

Debbie R.

He always comes into the kitchen limbering, not straight, bent away from the sunlight. He pours the black coffee into the big, chipped mug, peers at the rest of us over the rim, then says "Morning."

Mike R.

Every morning when I get up I think about her. Sometimes I think she's the only reason I come to school. The other day I watched her in the gym. They were practicing soccer. Ten girls were on one side of the gym, ten on the other. The coach would call out three girls' names and they would try to get the ball past the other team. Every time she ran back to her side of the gym she smiled and pushed the hair back from her eyes, shy and not really looking but knowing I was there.

Kirk F.

I've watched the laugh lines grow deeper, longer, and how her eyes begin to strain when she reads a book late at night, and how she stops now to rub the pain from her hands when she works the dirt around the flowers.

Jessie M.

He has a nervous way of strutting and showing off his muscles. Every-time he passes a window he puffs up his chest and looks out of the corner of his eye to see his reflection. He checks other people's mus-cles too, to make sure his are bigger. I'd love to tease him about it but I'm afraid to.

Alan M.

My father's string tie is loose. One foot is up on the couch, the other is on the floor. The midmorning sun lights his squinted eyes and drawn brow. Carefully chosen words come out on an extra push of air as he whispers his sermon to the congregation in his mind.

Rosemary B.

The other day Mom was watching her favorite soap opera. Suddenly she had tears in her eyes. She stood up, walked out of the room, came back with a tissue, wiped her eyes and involved herself again.

Dorraine R.

One thing these excerpts have in common is that none sounds as if it came from material uncovered in a reference book. These *are* fresh and orig-inal glimpses of live people. They reveal what one writer has seen and remembered. Furthermore, they spark our imaginations. It isn't hard to see Uncle Charlie, to feel you know what kind of person he is. And Todd's grandmother is instantly likable in her coveralls and "crimpled, dusty hat." All of these brief selections grant their subjects a life beyond the sentences themselves.

Something else about these pieces suggests an important truth about writing too: that it needn't be *objective*. Much attention is given to objectivity in classrooms and textbooks. We're reminded frequently to stick to the facts—to keep our feelings and opinions out of the writing in most situations. Assignments dealing with the famous dead, for example, usually leave little room for the writer. For young writers especially, this can be both difficult and frustrating. It isn't natural to write about matters that exist only outside of us—subjects that we have no part in discovering; assignments that deny us the chance to get what's inside of us outside.

For all the fuss that's made about being *objective,* it's a nearly impossible aim, no matter what you're writing about. Outside the small world of dry facts, there's nothing much you can know without getting yourself directly involved in the knowing. Knowing is a largely personal process, and you belong right in the middle of it. So don't worry about being objective. Worry instead about keeping yourself involved. Look at these pieces again. What's best about them—what makes them strong—is that in each case the writer, not just the information, shows. Who else could have seen as gently and affectionately how the girl shyly brushed back her hair and smiled? How could "objective" writing have made clear Jessie's loving concern about her mother? There are few cold facts in Rosemary's sketch of a moment in her minister father's life.

A final point to consider before you start your own writing is that each of these excerpts offers us only a small specific, a glimpse at a scene that existed just for a moment or two and probably would escape the notice of anyone other than the writer. People are made up of such moments, just under the bigger thing we label "life." When such moments are caught on paper, as they have been here, the subjects begin to breathe. Give the reader only generalized observations, the kind nearly anyone could make, and nobody breathes.

Who should you write about? Try someone close to you. That's what these writers did. List two or three possibilities, if you haven't already made up your mind. Make each name a column heading. Then jot down at random whatever comes to mind under each name. It won't take long to determine who's pulling at you hardest. Make up your mind at the beginning that you're not going to attempt a full biography. You won't prove to a reader how your subject is different—more likable or amusing or fascinating (or even obnoxious)—from all the rest of us by listing date and place of birth, or when he or she graduated from elementary school or broke a leg. Don't, in other words, try to *cover* the subject; be delighted instead if you can *uncover* it in a few small particulars.

When you're done, ask your writing group to read and respond. Also make a copy of the piece and give it to the person you chose for a subject. (Not, of course, if you've been pretty negative all the way through.) Whether or not they admit it, people love to be written about. If you decide to share your sketch, I can guarantee that the person you have written about will appreciate it—and ask you for a copy to keep.

21

Writing with Scissors

If one note sounded good and the other sounded good, I'd let the two of
them stay together. Then maybe I'd put another one along with them.

Alberta Hunter

The last place most of us look for something to write about is in someone else's writing. Something about words locked into print suggests that
what they say is the only way to say it, and now that it's been said the subject
is exhausted. Words in textbooks, newspapers, magazines, even fiction,
seem to be final, unchangeable. So we read, accept or reject the information,
and turn to other affairs.

As you move more deeply into writing, though, you're probably going
to discover that what words in print say is rarely final—that every article,
chapter, story is just one writer's way of understanding and dealing with a
subject. And in most cases the writer knows perfectly well that she hasn't
finished; she has just stopped. It isn't only your writing that you'll learn to
re-see; you'll also begin to sense that others' writing too can be recast, its
subject rediscovered and approached from your point of view, in your
voice. Sooner or later writers add a pair of scissors to their basic equipment
and use them to cut out articles that someday may provide a likely subject
for a piece of their own.

Here's one from my file. To me it suggested three possibilities: a children's story, a poem, and a memory piece, the last because I'd come on such a
sight the summer before while walking down a dirt lane deep in the woods.
What does it suggest to you? Maybe nothing at first, but bring your imagination to bear on the article anyway; try to find your own way into its subject,
not as a means to write an article that sounds at all like this one, but instead to
use it as the core of something quite different and entirely your own. If nothing seems to be coming, don't reject the basic idea here—that someone
else's writing can be the starting point for your own.

Prudent Spiders Weave Keep-Off-the-Web Sign

By Bayard Webster

Two species of spiders weave what amounts to signs saying "Keep Off
the Web" to prevent birds and large insects from damaging their prop-

erty, two Cornell University researchers have found.

Dr. Thomas Eisner, a biologist, and Stephen Nowicki, an animal behaviorist, report that they have observed loosely spun bands or patches of thick, white silk strands laid out across the center of the spiders' circular webs.

The extra strands, called stabilimenta by entomologists, make the webs many times more visible. Until now, however, scientists had not known why the spiders added such strands.

While observing the spiders in Florida, Dr. Eisner noted that songbirds hunting aerial insects would change their flight direction abruptly just before making contact with the ornamented webs.

Spiders Did Lasting Work

The researchers noted that the only types of spiders that wove extra-visible strands into their webs were those that spun durable webs that persisted through the day. Other types of spiders construct their webs in the evening and take them down at dawn.

The two types that added warning markers to their webs and were observed by the researchers are Argiope florida, a little-studied species, and Argiope aurantia, commonly known as the golden orb weaver spider, which inhabits meadows in the eastern United States.

Dr. Eisner suspected that the stabilimenta served as markers to warn off birds that fly in daylight that might otherwise tear through the webs.

He also theorized that, while it was of obvious benefit to spiders to protect their webs against destruction, the birds themselves profited by heeding the warning markers. Flying into the webs not only startled the birds but also left them contaminated with the sticky threads, requiring extensive preening.

Durability of Webs Compared

To test these theories, the researchers compared the durability of 30 natural webs without stabilimenta, used as controls, and 30 comparable webs that were ornamented with the thick white threads.

They found that while only about 6 percent of the nonmarked webs survived in a 12-hour period, more than 60 percent of the more visible webs remained intact.

The researchers also noted that most of the webs were destroyed by birds that accidentally flew into them.

Dr. Eisner, in a paper in the Jan. 14 issue of Science, said the findings also indicated that the highly visible webs of the spiders might also deter large ambulatory animals as well as large butterflies, which were seen to change direction abruptly in front of the marked webs and fly over them.

*   *   *

Ever since I first read the piece that follows I've been drawn back to it. It has resulted in two separate poems and a dialogue piece, and I doubt that I'm done with it now. Perhaps its somewhat stuffy tone or technical language or its age will leave you cold. Perhaps, though, after a couple of readings you'll find something in it too, as you could have in the article about spider webs.

The bridge that's written about here was built in 1792 across the Mohawk River in central New York State, then mostly wilderness. It was put up by settlers on both banks who worked on it on Sundays, the only day they could take away from farming and other work. It had been in use about a year when it was visited by Mark Brunel, a highly regarded engineer. Because Brunel *was* an engineer, he was used to looking at things with a technical eye. After reading his response two or three times, you should be able to sense some circumstances he overlooked or failed to understand. Try writing your own version, seeing the matter from your point of view, not Brunel's. You'll have to use your imagination. There aren't any facts beyond those describing the bridge itself and the brief conversation. It's the imagining that this piece provokes, however, that makes it so interesting, for me at least. Your writing can take any form that seems appropriate to you, but don't just re-state Brunel's writing. If you think pictures will work better than—or with—your words, draw pictures.

This bridge, built after the English manner, is in the arc of a circle, with a very moderate curve, and is supported by beams placed like St. Andrew's cross, and covered with plank. The bridge has already bent from the curve intended and inclined to the oval, an effect due as much to the framing as to the quality and smallness of the timbers, which are of pine and fir. The main support, which they have put in the middle, would rather tend to its entire destruction when the ice is going off. The abutments are of timber, and also settled from miscalculation of the resistance, the one on the south side being built upon ground that is full of springs.

This bridge has been built but a short time, and was erected by a country carpenter. We asked Mr. Post why, when they had such a work to execute, they did not employ an engineer or architect to draw a plan and the details, which a carpenter might then easily execute. He replied that this was not the custom, and that no carpenter would be willing to work after the plans of another man. He, however, appeared mortified at the probable fate of his bridge which we predicted.

[Note: The bridge went down in a flood not too long after Brunel's visit.]

One of the poems I wrote in reaction to the piece follows:

> We thought to build our own,
> And trust that honest work
> Will hold against a flood.
> Rather that than use
> Another's plan.

There was the creek; now here
Sits the span. I've not
Seen any pause in fear to cross,
Have you?

We snaked the logs down that
Third hill with Benson's team
And drew them to the mill,
And squared some to timbers
And all the rest to planks.

She ought to stand; all so
Far has, no thanks to engineers,
Who only trust a timber dry
Of sap.

Hell, give any building here
A rap and wall or floor
Will spit at you. It isn't just
This bridge; the *country's* raw
And green.

If we guessed wrong—if that
Support gives out, I mean—
Well, we did our best,
And so will do our best
Again.

It's our river, Sir.
It goes against the grain
That any dreaming architect
Should ink our way across.
We made this bridge; we'll risk
Its loss.

*   *   *

If you're ever stuck for something to write about (which shouldn't be the case anymore), go to your local post office and browse through the wanted posters—the descriptions, usually with a "mug shot," of wanted criminals. If you see them the right way, some of these pictures are fascinating "stories" in themselves. For a writer they're rich pickings. Don't leave just yet, however. First, react to what follows the way you've been asked to react to the other two pieces in this chapter.

This is a ballad, and it's based on an actual murder committed by Henry Green, who in 1845 poisoned his bride of a week, Mary Wyatt, in Berlin, New York. Because it was such an apparently heartless crime, there was much public outrage, along with sympathy for the young victim. At least seven ballads were written about the incident, along with some shorter poetry. While this ballad tells the story of the murder, it's one person's way of understanding the story. There are others. Respond to this writing (which, I admit, isn't great poetry) by bringing your own point of view to bear on the matter. Maybe you'll create your own poem, or you may choose to approach it in another form, perhaps a short story or a dialogue between Mary and Henry, or even a defense attorney's argument in Henry's behalf. See what happens. (At the time of the trial a printed picture titled "The Murdered Wife" was circulated. Does the ballad suggest some sketching? Even a cartoon? You might decide to set the piece to music. Originally it was meant to be sung.)

Mary Wyatt

Come, listen to my tragedy
Good people young and old,
An awful story you shall hear.
'Twill make your blood run cold;
Concerning a fair damsel—
Mary Wyatt was her name—
She was poisoned by her husband
And he hung for the same.

Mary Wyatt, she was beautiful,
Not of a high degree,
And Henry Green was wealthy
As you may plainly see.
He said, "My dearest Mary,
If you'll become my wife
I will guard you and protect you
Through all this gloom of life."

"O Henry, I would marry you;
I would give my consent,
But before that we'd been married long
I fear you would repent;
Before that we'd been married long,
You'd make me a disgrace
Because I'm not as rich as you
Which ofttimes is the case."

"O Mary, dearest Mary,
How can you grieve me so?
I'll vow and 'clare by all that's fair
I always will prove true;
But unless you consent to become my wife
You'll surely end my life
For no longer do I wish to live
Unless you are my wife."

Believing what he said was true,
She then became his wife.
But little did she think, poor girl,

That he would end her life.
O, little did she think, poor child,
And little did he explain
That he would end her precious life
And coldly watch it drain.
They had not been married but a week or two
When she was taken ill.
Great doctors were sent for
To try their powerful skill;
Great doctors were sent for
But none of them could save
And soon it was proclaimed
She must go to her grave.

O, when her brothers heard of this,
Straightway to her did go
Saying, "Sister dear, you're dying,
The doctors tell us so."
Saying, "Sister dear, you're dying;
Your life is at an end."
Saying, "Haven't you been poisoned
By the one you call your friend?"

"I'm on my deathbed lying.
I know that I must die.
I know I'm going before my God
And the truth I won't deny.
I know (my) Henry's poisoned me.
Dear brothers, for him send
For I love him now as dearly
As when he was my friend."

When Henry heard those tidings
Straightaway to his wife to see,
Saying, "Mary, my dearest Mary,
Was you ever deceived in me?"
Three times she called, "Dear Henry!"
Then and sank into a swoon.
He gazed on her indifferently
And in silence left the room.

"Now Henry has deceiv-ed me.
How my poor heart is wrong!
But when I'm dead and buried, O
Don't have poor Henry hung!
I freely have forgiven him,"
And she turned upon her side.
"In heaven meet me, Henry"
And she sweetly smiled and died.

*   *   *

Whether or not these pieces were the right ones to establish the value of re-seeing and reacting to other people's writing, begin a clip file rather than dropping the idea. Eventually, it will work for you. Make it a continuing part of your writing life.

22

Ouch

Writing is easy. I just open a vein and bleed.
Red Smith

The poem below was written by a young girl who had recently moved to a community far from her original home. As her poem so powerfully points out, she was at first treated cruelly by her new classmates:

Rejection
I
Walk up
And join
Them.
And they walk away.
Anne F.

Here's another statement concerning rejection, this one from a popular magazine. It is, in fact, an example of a "rejection letter" (although this one is not even a letter but a standard form), and writers who submit material for publication get them all the time. I have a shoe-box full.

Thank you for giving us the opportunity to consider the enclosed material. It has been read by members of the staff, and we are sorry that it is unsuited to our present needs. We regret, too, that the large amount of material we receive makes it impossible for us to offer individual comment.
The Editors

Now here's an 8th-grader's composition, before and after it was graded by his English teacher. Please read the "before" version slowly and carefully and only then look at the "after."

Some Thing I'll never forget

* I was. around 6 or 7 years old, when my fathers freind gave me a doller bill, probably the first I ever had. My mother kept in her pocket book in a plastic bottle, the kind you put pills in. I must have had that for years.

* One day my ma opend her pocket book, looked in it and got some money out to get some milk from the store. Down in town. Just then I looked in it and say something and there it was a big Back of wrigly gum. I wondered to my self how good that would taste in my noth.

* I decided I needed that gum put schould I steal it, This would have been the first time I ever stole anything in my life. I couldn't stand it no longer I wanted gum and Now. I impatiently sat down trying to thing of a way to get it. Racking my brains for hours I came up with an Idea.

a good Idea at that time.
Amediletly I put my plan in
action. I ran down stairs
found my mother and asked
can I see my dollar. She sat
there a while wondering why
I whanted to see my dollar.
She asked me and I said becau
She went in twice the room got
her pocket book off the closet and showed
me the dollar just then she danced
away for somthing. Then omedilaty
I took the gum, she turned around
asked me if I'm done. yes I
said she danced in her pocket book
and didnt see the gum where
is it she said. I sat there stuned
thingking now what can I do.
she bored out her junk looking
for it then I through the gum
in the pile of junk. lucky she
didnt hear me through it, she saw
the gum and said here it is.
I was releafed.

Alan—I had trouble reading this. It is filled with spelling errors and punctuation mistakes. Please be more careful about handwriting too—and watch those right-hand margins! As I've asked, write on one side of the paper only. (Spend more time on your writing. It looks as if you rushed through this.)

Some Thing I'll never forget   (capitalize)   MARGINS!

spell out numbers

. I was. around 6 or 1 years old, when my father's friend gave me a dollar bill, probably the first I ever had. My mother kept it in her pocket book in a plastic pill bottle, the kind you put pills in. I must have had that for years.

(wordy)

dollar for years

. One day my Mother opened her pocket book, looked in it and got some money out to get some milk from the store Down in town. Just then I looked in it and saw something there it was, a big pack back of wrigley gum. I wondered to my self how good that it would taste in my mouth?

(fragment)

. I decided I needed that gum put schould I steal it? It would have been the first time I ever stole anything in my life. I couldn't stand it no any longer I wanted gum and Now. I impatiently sat down trying to think of a way to get it. Racking my brains for hours I came up with an Idea.

(Run-on)

a good Idea at that time. (sp!) Amediletly I put my plan in action. I ran down stairs, found my mother and asked If I could can I see my dollar. She sat there a while wondering why I wanted to see it my dollar. She asked me and I said "because" She went into the room, got her pocket book from the closet and showed me the dollar. Just then she glanced? away for something. Then Amedilatly I took the gum, She turned around and asked me if I'm done. "Yes" I (Run-on) said, she glanced in her pocket book and didn't see the gum. Where is it she said. I sat there stuned thinking "Now what can I do.?" She bored out her junk looking (Run-on) for it, then I through the gun in the pile of junk. Lucky she (Run-on) didn't hear me through, she saw the gum and said Hear it is. I was releafed. sp (relieved) sp (Here)

As tempting as it is to point out the possible connections among these three items, it would be more meaningful for you to find them yourself. The poem, the form letter, and Alan's "Some Thing I'll never forget" are meant to be thought about, then discussed. Look in here for truths that should concern us first as humans, then more specifically as writers. Then deal with them in writing, any kind or form that seems best for saying what you understand and how you feel about these matters. There's no set "topic" here; you aren't limited to dealing with the three pieces in framing your response.

23

Still More Stuff

i

Almost every book that deals with writing has a section on grammar, although there's not much (if any) connection between the study of grammar and how and why we write. (Grammar study does have other importances, but unless you write sentences that come out looking like this: *Long the green crocodile the man's bit left leg,* you already know enough grammar to get by as a writer.)

Look up the definitions of the eight parts of speech in a grammar book. Jot them down; they're usually only a sentence long. You probably know them anyhow, but if you're like me, you've found them vague and misleading. The definition for *noun* is a good example. Usually it's put this way: *a noun is the name of a person, place, thing, or idea.* Isn't *Let's go downtown for a pizza* an idea? But it sure isn't a noun. The word *thing* is just as fuzzy. Here are cartoons that play with two of these definitions. Cook up at least two or more of your own, each dealing with a separate part of speech.

Adjective:

An adjective is a word used to modify a noun or a pronoun.

Here is a noun before it was modified:

And here it is after it was modified:

This kind of modifying normally costs about twenty dollars. If you know how, you can make a good living with adjectives.

Interjection:

An interjection is a word that expresses emotion and has no grammatical relation to other words in the sentence.

In the book I'm using for these rules, the authors offer these as examples of interjections: *Help! Wow! Whew! Gosh! Good grief!*
In the picture below, which of these interjections do you think the character is using?*

*If you aren't satisfied that any of the interjections above fits the situation, *do not*—repeat, *do not*—provide your own. It simply isn't necessary.

Parts of speech have a life above and beyond merely being labels for sentence elements. Cartoons provide one way of finding this life, but there are other ways as well. If you begin toying with the idea that the eight parts of speech have personalities—that possibly they're see-able, find-able, in a world beyond that of grammar books—you should be able to produce something memorable, either serious or humorous, about the one(s) you select to write about. Here are some examples. They're meant to set you thinking about possibilities of your own.

Noun

I found
An ancient noun
Rusting by
A broken wall.
The letters leaned
Together
Like tips
Of blowing grass
And sounded, when
I struck them,
Not at all.

Interjection

A shrewd old interjection
Raids the barnyard every night.
It howls "Good grief" and "Golly"
And gives the hens a fright.

My father wants to shoot it,
But No, my mother begs.
Without that interjection
We'd be buried in fresh eggs.

Verb

That silly verb
Is—get this!—
Telling birds—so help me—
How to *fly!*
As if a part of speech
Could reach the sky,
The way the very dumbest
Bird can do.

Adjective

You made that noun brown,
You clumsy, careless, sloppy clown.
Why splash yourself around
The one clean noun in town?

Adverb

How? When? Where?
To what extent?
Go ask your mother. Can't you see
I'm reading the paper?

ii

Maybe you're one of those people who's a terrible speller. If so, please write the following in huge red letters and post it over your desk: NO MATTER HOW YOU SPEL A MEWL IT WILL KIK YOU.

Being a weak speller should have nothing to do with how well you write. *Nothing.* Yet I've known students to freeze on paper when they've had the perfect word in mind but were afraid to put it down because they couldn't spell it. Some students become afraid to write *anything* for the same reason. *Get the word down any way you know how.* That's the important thing. Sure, the pressure's on you to spell correctly. Not just in school either. Misspelling is everywhere connected in readers' minds with ignorance, for reasons no one clearly understands. Eventually, every word should be spelled correctly. But it's a thousand times more sensible to use a word that seems right at the particular moment than it is to reject it because you're unsure whether the *e* comes before the *i* or, worse, to freeze up entirely because you've learned to be afraid of spelling. Later you can turn to the dictionary or ask an editor-friend to check out your spelling. That's one thing dictionaries (and friends) are for.

Will poor spellers ever become good spellers? There are rules and word lists to study. And there's a tendency for spelling to improve with reading and writing. But it's unlikely that a poor speller will ever become a spelling bee champion. As with much else in life, some people are naturally better at a skill than are other people. (And that's all spelling is—a *skill*, not an art or a mark of genius.) Even fairly good spellers have a pet list of words that in a lifetime they never learn to spell correctly, or that they have to stop and puzzle over. I nearly always write *conscience* when I mean *conscious*, and whether it's *discrete* or *discreet* continues to drive me crazy. I also use a dictionary several dozen times a day, and often it's to make sure I've spelled a word correctly.

Jot down a list of your own spelling demons. Don't worry about whether or not the words are spelled correctly; probably they won't be. Now use them, every one, in an unplanned ten or fifteen minute's worth of writing. The object is *not* to give you a new kind of spelling practice. It's to let you see that whether you spell it *mule* or *mewl*, it'll still kick.

iii

My daughter took a writing test administered by a very large retail sales company that relies heavily on catalogue advertising to sell its merchandise. Anyone applying for an editorial job in the catalogue division is required to take the same test. Applicants are asked to describe something they're wearing or carrying with them at the time—an article of clothing, jewelry, a cosmetic, even a pocketknife—in 300 words. This isn't a very tough challenge. There's no time limit, and within 300 words even a rookie should be able to say all there is to say about the chosen item.

What applicants don't know, though, is that when they finish the writing, they'll then be asked to say essentially the same things about the item—in just 30 words! (Count the words used to describe the typical catalogue item. Most write-ups run between 25 and 40 words. Catalogue advertising copy is extremely tight; not a word is wasted.)

You're invited to try your hand at this challenging test. It might work best if your entire group or even the whole class dealt with the same item and then compared notes. For a tougher version of this test, however, try this: each writer chooses a different item, writes up the 300-word description, and then swaps it with someone else to be boiled down to a tenth of its bulk. Try it either way. It's not merely a textbook exercise; it's a real-world challenge and effective enough to be used by one of the nation's largest merchandisers. My daughter said she thought it was one of the most challenging writing jobs she'd ever tackled. But she also said it was fun. (Before attempting this kind of writing, study closely and discuss the writing found in Sears and Montgomery Ward catalogues or publications of a similar nature.)

24

Lost and Found

I'm supposed to be writing about a year ago, but this pen doesn't go back that far.

Harold Decker

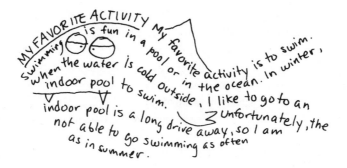

MY FAVORITE ACTIVITY My favorite activity is to swim. Swimming is fun in a pool or in the ocean. In winter, when the water is cold outside, I like to go to an indoor pool to swim. Unfortunately, the indoor pool is a long drive away, so I am not able to go swimming as often as in summer.

ENGFISH

My vacation was really interesting. We all had a great time. The drive was the most fun because we saw a lot of fascinating things along the way, like the Atlantic Ocean and the Ozark Mountains. Etc., etc.

I rode my horse to the mountin and a haawk kiled a rabit. I saw the rabit in front of the hourse the haawk came down on top of the rabit it made a skeeck sound. I did not no haawks are so big. It scare my horse and me to. I told my father he said it was a red tale haawk. It hoped with the rabit in his claw then it flew away. I saw the rabits blood on the grass.

In the second piece the punctuation's off, the spelling's terrible, and one sentence is out of order. But the writing is loaded with action and detail. It makes the reader pay attention from the start. Look at that first sentence again. The action starts as soon as the writing begins. And we get a chance to know the author too. There's a live person in there. A truth about writing you should understand and remember is that if you like the writing, you like the writer, even if you're not always aware of it.

As for the first piece, it's just about impossible to develop any sense about the person who wrote it, or whether anybody did. I've seen thousands of pieces like this one, and I long ago began believing that they come out of a composition machine hidden in the basement of nearly every secondary school. Put a quarter in, punch the "My Favorite Vacation" button, and plop, out comes a composition like this one. We should all, of course, be writing like the second author—not with the mechanical awkwardnesses that tell us the writer was a little kid, but with the eagerness and confidence this piece leaps with.

Whether or not you think the writer in you is thumping along happily at this point and even if you haven't been near the composition machine for months, you should do a case study. Every writer should, and more than once in a lifetime. By examining closely your own writing—not just recent stuff but samples that come from years back—you can discover how you've understood yourself as a writer, how writing has figured in your life, and what has shaped you into the writer you are today. Most people who do case studies are surprised at what they find and don't regret having spent the time. A research project with you as the subject shouldn't be dull.

The raw material for your study should be your own writing. Although you may not know it, parents often tuck away their children's writing, especially the early work in large, wobbly letters on yellow paper. For case studies *all* writing should be considered—notes, letters, diaries, even homework—anything at all you wrote when you were younger, from early childhood up to yesterday. It will probably take some digging, and you may come up with only a few clues. You'll find something, however. (Two possibilities: often friends save letters you've sent; and you can also look on old report cards for teachers' comments about your writing.) As you do the digging, keep notes on what you find and what it tells you—and notes on the questions raised in the following paragraphs. Don't just read them and pass on.

To help you rediscover your roots as a writer, figure on talking to people too. Parents, previous teachers, classmates and friends—anyone who knew you as a writer—should be interviewed. Find out, for example, whether you liked to tell stories when you were small. Did you show an early interest in learning letters even before you went to school? Did you try to "write" even before you could spell? In school were you eager to write? By any chance does a teacher remember any particular piece you did, or at least the kinds of writing you most enjoyed? As a child, was part of your play writing? Did you ever go off alone with crayons and paper to make stories? Did anything you wrote get displayed on a bulletin board or refrigerator door?

Search your memory. Did any one person especially encourage your writing? Did someone or some experience discourage you? Over the years have subjects in which writing was important been your strongest? your weakest? Did anything you wrote get published in a school paper, literary magazine, newspaper? If so, try to remember how you felt about it. Do you remember feeling a particularly strong urge to write in response to a personal experience or event? In what grade or grades did you do the most writing? The least? Any in which you did almost none? What writing do you most (or least) like to do? Who do you write letters to? And if you kept a diary, even for a week, what kinds of stuff did you put into it? What do you remember having a difficult time with in writing? What frustrated you most? Did you ever write a story or poem for just one person? Did you like it when another read your writing aloud to a group? (And before you began this book when was the last time that happened?)

Your notes and clues are pieces of a profile to be fitted together into a fairly accurate picture of a particular writer. Think of them as being somewhat like the bones unearthed at Herculaneum that when examined closely forced a "revision" of past understandings. Your task won't be as complicated; the pieces should fit together fairly easily, although you may be a bit surprised at what they reveal. Probably the best format for your case study will turn out to be an autobiography. Not the kind that starts "I was born on January 7, 19—," but a work that focuses only on you as a writer. You'll be analyzing, not just recording. To do this, use the field-note approach as one technique for analysis. The earliest writings you've dug up, for example—if you'd found them in a trunk in someone's attic and didn't know who wrote them or anything else about the pieces, what might field-noting bring to light?

Don't overlook any clues or recollections—get them on paper. Jot down what others say. Consider seriously whether comments by parents, teachers, friends reflect your own feelings about yourself as a writer. You'll find that as you write, the writing itself will keep bringing back memories that you'd never find just staring out a window trying to recall.

You might find it useful and interesting to classify the types of writing you've done in terms of the purpose it served. Which of it seems to be the kind of writing you did mostly to please yourself—to hear and see yourself on paper? And which of it is for purposes and audiences that extend beyond you, such as school papers, messages, letters, explanations, directions, etc.? This should provide hints about such concerns as how you've written for yourself as compared to how you've written for other audiences; which types of writing seem to please you more; that indeed there *is* a difference in your voice on paper when you direct your words at others. Where are you able to find what seems to be the greatest degree of enthusiasm? Imagination? How do these compare with your more current areas of enthusiasm and imagination in writing?

More generally, can you trace the factor of growing up, getting older, as an influence in your writing? Not just in your ability to deal with more complicated subjects, but any major shifts or breaks in basic attitudes about writing, or in writing habits. In other words, have any really important changes occurred? Or are you still basically the same writer grown older?

25

Writers on Writing

No writer has ever lived who did not at some time or other get stuck.
Donald Murray

Some people think that the best way to learn how to write is to read about how others do it. I'm not sure. Writers seldom agree with one another about writing methods. To some, the color of the ink is important, or the time of day. Ray Bradbury starts every day by writing a poem. Ernest Hemingway did much of his writing standing up, and Winston Churchill often wrote in bed, as did Mark Twain. I know a couple of writers who will not write in longhand at all but insist on typing from the start, yet other writers I've talked with believe that to be an impossible method. They prefer scrawling on long yellow pads and then going back and typing the results. A very few well-known writers dictate, either to a secretary or into a machine. Ex-President Jimmy Carter uses a word processor instead of a typewriter, and quite a few writers have said that this method is extremely efficient. (Just as many, though, can't stand the idea.) A close friend and very fine writer does no rough drafting, except in his head. What he finally puts on paper is what he feels to be the finished sentence. This seems terribly difficult to me, but it works for him.

Here are a few things that writers—good ones, anyhow—agree on.
- There's no one right way to write.
- Writing is difficult (and stays that way).
- It isn't always necessary to have a set plan before you start to write.
- Writing takes self-discipline, not genius. Because writing *is* hard work, it's tempting to hide from it. (One Pulitzer Prize-winning writer told me that his way of hiding is to drive downtown and buy fresh supplies of ballpoint pens. Another writer friend says that he sits in his office waiting for the phone to ring, and that if it doesn't, he invents reasons for calling people. Hemingway recommended defrosting the refrigerator.) The discipline is in not hiding but writing.
- All writers suffer occasionally from "writer's block." Nothing happens; no decent lines come. This is not a dread disease; it only feels like one. Usually, writer's block disappears within a day or two.

- No piece of writing, regardless of how much you polish and fuss with it, comes out exactly as you want it to. It's never a matter of "perfect"; it's a matter of the writer's deciding when the work is finally *good enough.*
- Sometimes—often, in fact—a piece of writing never gets good. No writer expects to bat a thousand, or even .300.

Maybe some (or even all) of these truths don't relate to your experience so far. Perhaps you may even be thinking something like, "Why all this talk about professional writers? I'm a student, not a writer." In a couple of respects you're right. There are differences between you and the professional: for one thing, you don't have the necessary time to spend. (Most professionals are satisfied if they can produce 1½–2 pages of decent work by the end of a full day.) For another, you don't get paid for what you write (unless you're very fortunate).

But let me argue that whenever you work honestly at writing, you're a writer, whether or not you're earning money at it. The label "student writer" bothers me. It suggests that neither you nor anyone who reads your stuff is meant to think of it as being *real*; that instead it should be looked at as some kind of practice, or simply as another school requirement that people take for granted, like learning multiplication tables. This isn't true, or shouldn't be anyhow. By now, something you have written may even be "professional"—good enough to be shared with a much wider audience than classmates and teacher. It doesn't necessarily take years for a writer to turn pro.

And what you have to *say* about writing, even though your methods may not work for somebody else, can be just as interesting and authentic as the observations of a professional on the subject. To let others know how you feel about writing and how you go about it should demonstrate to you that you already know much about yourself in the writer's role; and even if your discoveries don't prove directly useful to another, they're almost bound to make for interesting listening and reading.

The interview provides an excellent way to get a writer to loosen up and talk about him- or herself and the subject of writing. You've seen countless interviews on TV, mostly on news and talk shows. Here's an example of an interview, a printed version of a conversation in which the interviewer asked his subject a series of questions, one at a time, and let the subject do most of the talking.

A Few Thoughts About Writing
with Andy Rooney

Andy Rooney began his journalism career as a correspondent during World War II. After the war, he became a radio and television writer for some of the major figures in early TV, including Garry Moore and Arthur Godfrey. Later, Mr. Rooney began to present his own TV material in such acclaimed specials as *Mr. Rooney Goes to Washington, Mr. Rooney Goes to Dinner,* and *Mr. Rooney Goes to Work.*

At present, Andy Rooney can be seen weekly on *60 Minutes,* where he provides insightful observations on topics ranging from clothing tags to army tanks. And he can be read three times a week in a syndicated column, which appears in 222 newspapers. He has written five books, the latest of which, *A Few Minutes with Andy Rooney,* is a bestseller.

[Here] Mr. Rooney offers the following observations on his writing and on writing in general.

How would you describe the way you go about writing one of your columns?

If I have an idea, I sit down and start typing. If I don't have an idea, I sit down and decide to have one. When I have one, I start typing. When I have written about 600 words, I stop, read it over, and more often than not, rewrite it.

Are you ever troubled with writer's block?

I don't have writer's block much. If I do, it's usually because I'm thinking about something else, not about what I ought to be writing. Too many writers wait to be struck by an idea. If they aren't struck by one, they think they have writer's block. This isn't the way it works. I sit down and decide to *get* an idea. If I don't get one after trying, that's writer's block. It seldom happens.

How do you pick the subjects you write about, and is it getting harder to think of new ones?

I don't pick subjects so much as they pick me. Ideas seem to present themselves to me all the time. It is not getting harder to think of ideas, although I sometimes get tired of the format I use. _ *Bill — a formula?*

How much mail do you get from *60 Minutes'* viewers? Can you generalize about the letters you receive?

I get several hundred letters a week. My *60 Minutes* mail comes to the office and my column mail comes home. It is more than I can read, let alone answer. I feel bad about it. I used to think that writing a letter was its own reward and that fan mail should be thrown out, unopened. I've softened on that. Some of the mail is not only very nice but often interesting. I see most of the interesting things. Mail breaks down into about five categories:

1) Nice

2) Idiotic (religious, political, etc. These are usually six pages, handwritten on both sides with something they forgot written on the outside of the envelope).

3) Requests—for scripts, for my autograph, for a homework interview from a sixth grader, for something of mine to be auctioned off for a good cause. I throw most of these out unanswered.

4) Old friends from other segments of my life. We all make more friends than we keep, and it's nice that I'm visible enough for old friends to find me. It's one of the few good things about well-known-ness.

5) Ideas, poems, one glove, soap, an invention, cute PR letters trying to attract my attention to some shoddy promotion.

In your writing and TV appearances, you come across as easy-going, unhurried, and just a trifle disorganized. However, the amount of work you obviously do implies self-discipline and a lot of rushing around. Is the image of easy-going disorganization pretty much a fiction?

I just had my blood pressure taken and it was 120 over 80. I tense up quickly but I come back down quickly. I can nap. The only discipline I have ever imposed on myself is the one that enables me to get the most done: I get up in the morning whether I feel like it or not. Nothing more than that. It is the only difficult or unpleasant thing I face. I get up at 5:45 every single day and catch a 6:13 train to New York. This gives me confidence that even if I'm slow or unproductive, I can stay even with everyone else and probably get ahead of most of them.

Do you have any pet peeves about the writing of today?

My peeves change. For several years I enjoyed hating the misuse of the word *infer*, but hating that got so popular that I dropped it. For a short while after that, I was irritated by the misuse of the word *comprise*, but now I've settled on the infuriating and ubiquitous *s* on the end of so many words that are perfectly good singulars. I haven't read of anyone having *skill* and *talent* in years. They all have *skills* and *talents*.

There's been a lot written lately about how students' writing is deteriorating. Do you have any thoughts about that?

Writing is deteriorating for the same reason Americans are doing everything else that's difficult poorly. It's easier to fake with the spoken word because you don't have to be precise. You can pretend to mean more than you're saying. You can pretend you're being profound and force on the listener the necessity for nodding or saying "yeah" as if he understood. If you can't put down an idea on paper, the chances are you don't have an idea.

Teaching writing is difficult, and I suppose that many teachers emphasize form over content because grammar is closer to arithmetic and easier to mark right or wrong. Content ought to be the first consideration of any teacher of writing. Teachers should teach petty points of usage only when they help students understand nuances of expression.

Have you ever taught writing?

I've lectured in writing classes at Columbia, Syracuse, Yale, the University of Iowa and NYU. Whether I ever taught anyone anything is unknown to me.

Are you ready to be interviewed? Good. You'll also conduct an interview of your own, of course. This way, everyone in your group will be both interviewer and subject. Among you, work out the basic details about who will interview whom. Unless you're very good at taking notes, a cassette recorder will prove useful. (You may find yourself freezing or getting very nervous when someone thrusts a microphone at you. Don't worry; the feeling goes away in a couple of minutes.) A quiet setting is essential, and so is a serious intention to bring out as much information as possible. Keep in mind that this is for others. It's neither exercise nor play.

People being interviewed often react in one of two different ways, wandering endlessly or mumbling a few words and then clamming up. As an interviewer, be prepared for either circumstance; be ready to steer the wanderer back on course with something like "Shall we go to another subject?" and with the clam to keep rephrasing the question and pressing for more information. A technique that many interviewers use is the "off-camera warm-up," a relaxed chat with the subject before the button is pushed and the recording starts.

Plan on at least a half-hour for the interview, maybe more. You probably won't end up talking and listening that long, but pre-interview conversation, interruptions, and false starts will gobble up time. Make a brief test run to determine the best position for the recorder. Be sure that it's not too close or too far from you and the subject.

You'll almost certainly know your subject fairly well, and this can lead to the kinds of personal questions that make an interview come alive. "How do you manage to concentrate on writing with three brothers and two sisters in the house?" or "You're an athlete. Have you ever written about sports?" are the kinds of questions that can produce relaxed, informative answers.

Here are some other questions, any or all of which you can reject in favor of your own. Plan a set of questions in advance, however, and also be prepared to depart from them if your subject moves into an interesting area you hadn't counted on covering.

- Tell me about yourself as a writer as far back as you remember. Can you relate a couple of early writing experiences that stand out?
- What do you think has changed for you regarding writing? Do you think, for example, that you're developing a style of your own? How would you describe it?
- What's your favorite form of writing—essay, letter, poem, journal? Why?
- Who (or what) has been the biggest influence on your writing?
- Do you think you're a "natural" writer—someone who has a built-in talent that makes writing easy? Or do you have to work hard at it to produce something good?

- Do you always know what you're going to write before you write it?
- Do you show your writing to others as you develop a piece?
- Do you ever hide from writing? What kinds of excuses do you use?
- How do you know when a piece of your writing is good and when it's not?
- How about your methods? Tell me how you get ready for writing—where you go, what you need to have, how you get started—things like that.
- Have you ever suffered from writer's block?
- When you write, do you ever compose in your head? That is, do you try to write a sentence or a paragraph before you actually put it on paper?
- On the average, how many versions (or drafts) of a piece do you go through before you figure it's done?
- When you're not satisfied with something you've just written, do you try changing it or are you more likely to put it aside or throw it out?
- What kind of writing do you *hate* to do?
- What kind of writer do you most respect—a reporter, a novelist, a poet, etc.? Can you name a writer, living or dead, you'd most like to write like?
- If you had the chance to give others any advice about writing, what would you tell them?
- Are you working on a piece right now? If so, what can you tell me about it?
- Do you think you'll write all your life, aside from occasional letters or paperwork that might be connected to your job?
- Do you ever think about someday becoming a professional writer?

Transcribing the interview—getting it down on paper—will take time and care. Figure on editing; when you listen to the recording or look over your notes, you'll almost certainly find that some of the questions didn't produce useful, interesting responses. You'll probably also find that even those questions that did bring forth good answers may also be wordy, long-winded. Save those parts of your subject's comments that really say something, and throw out the rest. There's nothing wrong with transcribing two or three lines from an answer that might run twenty lines if you copied it down, so long as the two or three lines you save hit the heart of the question. The rest might just be empty chatter. You be the judge. It will pay you to listen to the recording two or three times before you start transcribing. This is the time to weed out the useless material, not after you've gone to the trouble of copying it all down on paper.

I've found that the best way to transcribe is to play just enough of the recording to remember and jot it down in quick form. At the same time try to hear the punctuation of it, so that as you copy you'll be converting your subject's words into written language, with the necessary signals for the reader. (If you can get a volunteer to help you, fine. You can offer to help in return.)

You're probably going to run into problems you didn't notice during the interview. Unless your subject had all his or her answers written down or memorized before your talk (which isn't a good idea), the recording will be peppered with *ahh's* and *umm's*, to say nothing of giggles. You may also notice that some sentences will be broken in the middle or may just stop dead. These and other odd little hitches can mostly be edited out as you transcribe. But if you think that a chuckle at a certain point adds something to the statement, put the word *laughter* in parentheses at the appropriate point. And if a key sentence stops in the middle, end it by using four periods instead of one.

Finally, you'll need a clean copy. If possible, have it typed. Maybe you can enlist a family member. If not, at least produce the neatest-looking piece of writing you've ever accomplished. And use black ink. It works best for machine copying. These interviews should definitely be given to their subjects and should also be bound together as a book. Call it *Writers on Writing* or *Writers Talking About Writing,* or whatever; just make sure that somehow it becomes a one-volume collection and that it also gets placed in the library after everyone has had a chance to read it.

Do you know a professional writer, a newspaper reporter, poet, advertising copywriter, or editor, for example? Why not interview him or her? For that matter, why not interview anyone in the community who spends time at writing, whether it's someone who writes children's stories for a hobby or is writing a community history, or even collecting *others'* writings—journals, letters, for example?

Nearly all writers claim to be terribly busy. And they are. Yet it usually isn't difficult to get one to talk about writing, at least for a few minutes. Quite often a writer is willing to talk on paper, especially to someone who seems honestly interested and eager to learn. Have you ever considered writing to a writer whose work you enjoy? Probably not. Somehow we come to believe that well-known people are unwilling to bother with the likes of us—that requests for information or pictures or autographs will end up in wastebaskets.

Sometimes this is what happens, but not as often as you might expect. A good letter begs to be answered, no matter who it's from. Perhaps more than most other busy, well-known people, writers feel drawn to respond to writing. Therefore, consider choosing a writer or two and sending him or her a letter, the kind that makes a reader want to write back. Believe me, it doesn't take a special genius to write an honest-sounding, this-deserves-an-answer kind of letter. It only takes your putting in your own friendly voice why you're writing and stating exactly what you want. Because you're young, don't try to sound adult; because you're a student, don't attempt to sound like a college professor; in short, because you're you, don't try to write like someone else.

What *do* you want? You should have a fairly specific answer to this question in mind when you write. Read this letter from James Thurber, the late American humorist, to a couple of students:

West Cornwall,
Connecticut
March 17, 1958

Messrs. Dave Kussow and Tom Chopin
De Pere, Wisconsin

Dear Boys:

You can tell where I get my ideas from the things I write, and then you will know as much about it as I do. To write about people you have to know people, to write about bloodhounds you have to know bloodhounds, to write about the Loch Ness monster you have to find out about it. I write because I have to write and it's a good thing a writer gets paid. If I juggled because I have to juggle I couldn't live. You will have to ask my readers why they read what I write. I hope they read it because it has something to say. You can also say that writers could get more written if they didn't have to answer so many questions about why they write.

Best wishes.

Sincerely yours,
James Thurber*

By reading Thurber's response to these two students you can figure pretty closely what they must have asked. You can also note the writers' annoyance at the broad scope of the questions. Still, even though Thurber was irked, he offers a couple of amusing but valuable comments about his writing.

Put yourself in your reader's place. What would you do with a letter that asked, "Please tell me what you know about writing" (or "Will you please explain how you write?")? A polite but busy writer might answer by saying that your request is impossibly broad and vague; a less thoughtful writer would simply put such a letter where it probably belongs, in the wastebasket. A far more sensible request might be, "I'd appreciate knowing whether you ever find it difficult to sit down and write, and if you do, what is your favorite way to avoid it," or maybe, "I love to write, but sometimes I can't find a way to get started. Could you please let me know about any good ways you have discovered?" These examples are meant to demonstrate the difference between a hopelessly fuzzy request and answerable ones. Form your own questions. Don't let *my* words get into *your* letter.

I do have a couple of ideas that you may want to borrow and put into your own words.

- Why not ask a writer whose writing you like to spend three or four minutes scribbling down the first things that come to mind about the word *writing*? Few people are too busy to spend that little time, especially if you make clear that it isn't a midget essay you want, just quick

*from *Selected Letters of James Thurber,* edited by Helen Thurber and Edward Weeks. (Boston: Atlantic-Little, Brown, 1980) p. 198.

unplanned impressions. If this idea appeals to you, be sure to include a promise that you won't publish your writer's response, that it's just for classmates and family to share.

- Request that a writer fish out of his or her wastebasket a scrap of writing that didn't work, or a small piece of rough draft that you would otherwise never have the chance to see in print. If you're fortunate, you may receive a clue as to how one writer goes about re-seeing ideas.

Whatever you choose to ask of your writer(s), here are a few basic tips on how to reach the envelope-licking point:

- It's better not to use ruled paper for stationery. For some reason, letter-readers are often put off by notebook or school-paper letters, possibly because it makes the letter look like an assignment rather than the real thing. I'd advise against the kind of note paper decorated with cute little animals or flowers too; plain white paper works best.
- Be sure to introduce yourself—but briefly. It's more or less expected that a letter from a stranger will include some personal information at the start. For example,

    I'm fourteen and a ninth-grade student at Corbin Central School. (Some people firmly believe that the first sentence of a letter shouldn't include the pronoun *I*. What this most often leads to is a first sentence that beats around the bush. My rule is simpler: Start the letter with a sentence that says what you mean to say. If there's an *I* in it someplace, fine.)

- Next, it would be a good idea to explain why you're writing, perhaps something like

    I've read two of your books, _____ and _____, and liked them very much. Although I'm studying writing at school, this letter isn't an assignment. I'm interested in writing and would appreciate your spending just a few minutes responding to a question (or request):

Now follow up with whatever it is you've decided you want to ask.

- When I request something in a letter, I usually end up by saying "Thanks. I look forward to hearing from you." If that sounds natural to you, use it. But put your closing comment in whatever way sounds friendly and comfortable to you. Many letter writers go stiff at the end, closing a request letter with a stuffy-sounding "Thank you for your kind attention to the above-mentioned request. I look forward to receipt of your reply at your earliest convenience." Don't ever write anything like that, unless you want to sound like an 18th-century lawyer (or a 20th-century lawyer).
- "Sincerely" is as good a final word to use in a letter to a stranger as any I can think of. Other so-called "complimentary closes"—"Your friend" or "Your biggest fan," for example—are too chummy for strangers to use with strangers.

Finding a writer's home or office address can be a real chore and is sometimes next-to-impossible. Fortunately, there's a fairly reliable way around this problem. Publishers are usually willing to forward letters addressed to their authors. (Book publishers are better about this than magazine publishers.) Publishers' addresses are easy to find. Magazines include this information, usually in small print, at the foot of an opening page. Be sure to write to their editorial or publishing address and not to a sales, distribution, or regional address. Most books do not list the publisher's street address, but the chances are that your librarian will have full addresses for most publishers. Occasionally, you'll be able to find an author's home town listed in a biography; if the place is small enough, you'll be safe sending your letter without a street address, just the writer's name, town, state and zip code. Another source for writers' addresses is *Who's Who in America.* If the writer who interests you has earned any fame, he or she will probably be listed in this directory, along with an address and some interesting highlights and background. Either your school or local library should have a copy.

To send your letter to a publisher for forwarding, be sure to place the author's name at the top, then directly beneath it "In care of" or its abbreviated form, "c/o." The publisher's address follows. Under this address print or type prominently "Please forward." Finally, don't forget to include your return address. Even better, include a self-addressed, stamped envelope. If the letter doesn't come back within a couple of weeks, your writer has received it.

One last, extremely useful tip: Be certain that the writer you choose is still alive. (It's highly unlikely that you'll get an answer from Edgar Allan Poe, Charles Dickens or Mark Twain. If you do, let me know.)

Good luck. If you don't get an answer from the writer you've chosen, don't be discouraged. Try again. You'll get an answer. And if you do nothing more with it than read it, share it, and tuck it away, the effort will have been worth it.

26

All Together and All Alone

When you have succeeded in establishing these two habits—early morning writing and writing by agreement with yourself—you have come a long way down the writer's path.

Dorothea Brande

The best place to write is away from noise and other forms of distraction. Being alone and unbothered won't automatically mean that whatever you write will be good, but it's hard to concentrate when people and noises press in from all sides. Unfortunately, a quiet setting can be tough to find. Many households swarm with people of all ages, all of them in their own way demanding space and contributing to the noises of home. Thus, writers often work in less than ideal circumstances, to the point where being alone in a quiet setting is at first more distracting than working in the middle of a familiar racket. As a writer, learn to seek out silences and treasure them. Even if you're at first bothered by the quiet company of a pen and blank paper, force yourself to respond. You'll find that with absolutely nothing intruding on you but your own determination to write, good things will start to happen. If you find a space and a time that are entirely your own, and you fill it with nothing but writing materials and your own good mind, you'll learn more about yourself as a writer than any book can tell you.

But what about the writing that must be done in school? Much of it takes place in a classroom where you're surrounded on four sides by others, scrunched behind an uncomfortable desk and interrupted by bells, buzzers, announcements, dropped books, hiccups, and giggles. Only writing inside a boiler factory could be worse. But maybe, aside from quizzes and exams that must be taken in the classroom, there are some kinds of writing and writing-related activities for which the classroom is ideal.

I hope that by now you've found that your classmates are valuable to you as editors, as fellow writers with whom to discuss problems and discoveries, and as audience for your work. But have you used one as the subject of a study of how a writer *looks* when she writes? Try it; it's fascinating. Each of us has a set of unconscious mannerisms that come into play when we write. Sketch a short word picture of a fellow writer, making careful notes about how your subject expresses the body language part of writing. Be sneaky; if a writer knows you're observing, self-consciousness will set in. After working your quick notes over into an accurate description, provide your subject with a copy. Here's an example of such a portrait:

> Marcia puts her whole body into her writing, from the top of her head all the way to her feet. Her left hand is always busy twirling the same lock of hair. First she pulls it loose, then she winds it around her finger. About five times she stopped hair twirling and chewed on her left thumbnail. This happened when she paused in her writing, so maybe the nail chewing means she's trying to come up with a key thought. The rest of her keeps moving too. She switches from sitting straight as a ramrod to practically lying down on her chair. There's no in-between position, it's one way or the other. It must be hard to write with her eyes just about level with the desktop, but she does it. Meanwhile, her feet are going too. When she slumps down she sticks her feet out in front and taps the toes together. When she sits up straight her feet go under the chair and she knocks her heels together. Marcia is very busy when she writes.
>
> *Betsy B.*

*   *   *

The word *poetry* can bring to mind a picture of a writer slaving away by candle-light in a lonely attic room. But not all poetry writing requires solitude or even deep concentration. Some kinds of poetry, in fact, lend themselves to group writing. (Not that you can't accomplish them alone as well.) Ever try making a poem of your own name? Form a small group—four or five of you at most—and take turns developing a name poem for each of you. Put down a group member's name, placing each letter on a separate line. Each person, including the one named, should then find a word beginning with each letter. The words should somehow describe or characterize the name's owner. (Being insulting is not, of course, the object.) Keep word choices to yourself until all of you have completed the "poem." It won't take that long, especially if you put down the first words that come to mind— they're often the best. Now compare terms and, without getting too fussy about it, settle on a combination of choices that seems best to capture the person named. Here are two examples:

Mellow
Arguments
Romantic
Yodels

Talking
Articulate
Never
Never
Empty
Rhymes

Jolly
Oddball
Energy

Ridiculous
Orange
Sagging
Sweater

Note: Working either with your own or another's name you can also come up with an amusing name poem by skimming the dictionary for especially weird words. This isn't the time to worry about definitions; it's the sound and shape of the word that count.

A name poem needn't involve someone's description or characteristics. An interesting challenge is to work at making a meaningful poem while sticking with a name's first letters:

> The old man,
> Odd to say,
> Died just the other
> Day
>
> Because he was forced to
> Untie his tie and
> Retire from his job.
> Ready and willing, no
> One would let him
> Work.
> Sad.

Have you ever heard of a *cinquain*? It's a five-line poem in which the first line has one word; the second, two words; the third, three words; the fourth, four words, and the fifth, one word. You can do round-robin cinquains in a group. Each person puts a first word on paper, then passes it to the next person. If there are four people in the group, you get to provide the last word too. With five people, someone else finishes what you began. Either way the results are usually interesting and/or amusing. Here are a couple of group-written cinquains:

> One   Green
> Two, three   Is water
> I count impatiently.   Running coldly over
> The minutes crawl by   Moss and bent weeds
> Reluctantly.   Swaying.

Working individually or in a group you can find poems in unlikely places. "Found poetry," which is what some people call this kind of writing, is just that: poems made up from single words and phrases found by rooting through various kinds of prose such as newspapers and magazine articles, the yellow pages of a phone book, even a textbook. The only "rule" connected with writing found poems is that you should try sticking to one article (or page) for your raw material. The following poems were "found" by writers who assembled them from single articles in one issue of a daily paper:

> Two people awake in Rhodesia,
> A tornado in their minds
> Of Yuletide accidents,
> Crooked politicians
> And four-day weekends.

Holidays in the Rocky Mountains,
Turkey-and-trimmings dinners—
A violent storm battles in their brains,
A thousand kilowatts of power
Ready to emerge.

Joe B.

Someone toward the sky
Dots the landscape from
Cork to Derry,
Where lavishly costumed
Lords and ladies
Flock from mainland Europe
And Irish jets
Capture your heart.

Danny S.

The amusing—and remarkable—thing about found poems is that although they're collections of scattered words and phrases arranged in ways their original authors never intended, they nearly always seem to make some kind of quite new sense. Writers working with found poetry usually say that a clear picture begins to form for them as they pluck these elements from their original sources. Thus, it isn't just a matter of copying someone else's words; it's finding new meaning in them.

Still another kind of poem lends itself to co-authoring too. Two writers provide alternate lines or stanzas of a poem, either agreeing at the start on a subject and/or format or simply letting the poem find a meaning and shape of its own as the lines build. Here are two such co-authored works:

There are times when
I love sheep but hate wool,
I hate fire but love candlelight,
I love to be secluded but hate to be alone,
I hate small children but love kids,
I love jokes but hate riddles,
I hate darkness but love black,
I love soda but hate fizz,
I hate mirrors but love reflections,
I love books but hate reading,
I hate fudge but love chocolate, and
I love the world but hate to be in it.

Karen A. and Gail V.

And everyday I
Wished for bright umbrellas
And big, round sunglasses,
And for millions of dollars
With nothing to buy.

And everyday I
Wished for long, quiet nights
And fireworks and white, white moons,
And for greens and blues and yellows
And snow coming down from gray skies.

And everyday I
Wished I could travel to a far country
And be standing here looking out the same window.

And one day I
Wished for the end of me
And didn't want to say goodbye.

Debbie D. and Mike W.

What other kind of writing lends itself to a classroom setting? How about scripts of three- or four-minute scenes from a novel or short story? a brief two-person comedy routine? round-robin story writing? circulating copies of cartoons with captions masked out to see who comes up with the best caption?

*   *   *

Just two more suggestions:

Is there a literary magazine in your school? Mostly, the answer to this question is *no*. While such projects can be costly and time-consuming, they needn't be. In fact, no school, regardless of size or funds, should be without such a publication. When good writing happens, it deserves to be published. And absolutely no school lacks the young writers to produce good writing. If you don't have a literary magazine, try producing your own, at least one experimental issue.

You'll need a title, of course, and it's a good idea to pick one first off. You'll also have to sniff out a free or very inexpensive source of printing, perhaps a school copying machine or one owned by a generous parent or business person in the community. Next you should find a typist, which shouldn't be difficult, especially since your first effort probably won't be too large. Paper can be provided by the school (or should be, anyhow; it doesn't cost that much and I can't think of a better purpose to put it to).

Whose writing should appear in such a publication? This is a tough question, maybe the toughest. Depending on your circumstances and your class's feelings (and also your teachers' and/or administrators' determinations), you can restrict this first effort to class members' writings or invite contributions from other classes of the same age, or throw it open to the whole school. The other end of this question is who chooses what goes in and what doesn't? Typically, a student editorial board is selected (or volunteers). At least one teacher should be involved too, in an advisory role. A final note on this matter: When you reject a piece, be gentle and courteous. No matter what shape it comes in, rejection hurts. Try to minimize another's pain. *Always.*

The simplest and least expensive format for such a publication is the standard 8½ × 11-inch sheet. Folded once the wide way, it will give you four pages, 5½ × 8½ inches. Just four of them and you'll have a 16-page magazine, an impressive first effort. Advise your typist to type single space, and you'll have enough room for a dozen shorter poems and a short story or two. Stapling the sheets together, either at the very top left corner or down the spine, will help to create a magazine-like appearance. So will a separate cover, although a simple printed or typed title on page one is the simplest way out, especially for a first, experimental edition.

Distribution is any publisher's major problem. By making the sensible decision to print too few, rather than too many, you'll have saved yourself time, maybe money, and the discouraging experience of being stuck with copies nobody seems to want. It's a basic truth about humans that people desire what is difficult to come by. Produce too many copies and you'll find them on corridor floors, in wastebaskets, left on schoolbus seats. Estimate how many you know will be snapped up by students, faculty, parents, community members, reduce your estimate by twenty percent and don't go beyond that number. Also don't leave stacks of your magazine in places where people can grab more than their share. Although you may not want to sell the publication, it's not wise to make it too free, either. That is, advertise your magazine, but ask interested people to *request* a copy, either in person or on a sign-up sheet.

The second suggestion isn't a class project exactly, but it relates to the literary magazine idea and may well grow out of it for a number of people in the class. I hope it does. You've probably never thought about giving your words as a gift, but think of all the people in your family—or even among your friends—who'd be delighted to receive a small, attractively bound collection of your poems, stories, or even selected journal entries. This is the kind of gift that others cherish for a lifetime. Creating the contents for such a work may not be simple, but binding them into book form is easy. The following instructions will show you how. (And by the way, it isn't necessary to limit this idea to gift-making. There are many other good reasons for binding words, yours and others'.)

You'll need fairly sturdy cardboard to form the book's covers. Cut two pieces, each 6″ × 9″. Next, choose an outside covering for the cardboard. Self-stick wallpaper, oilcloth, or light-gauge naugahyde all work well. Whatever you choose, cut a piece 11″ × 14″. Put the design-side down and lay the two pieces of cardboard on it, leaving just a slight amount of room between adjacent edges, as shown. If the covering you've selected is *not* the self-stick type, smear the downside of the cardboard with glue and weight them for awhile, until there's a firm bond between boards and covering.

Next, nip off the corners of the covering and fold over the excess. Glue that to the cardboard—even if it's self-stick—but not until you're satisfied that your folding is as neat and flat as possible. Cut the two cover halves apart with a single-edge razor blade. Make your cut down the narrow margin you left between the two pieces of cardboard. Then line up the two

pieces, keeping the covered sides down, so that there's approximately ¼"
between the edges you've just cut. Cut a piece of Mystik tape (or similar
sturdy tape) 9" long and tape the two pieces together on the inside, main-
taining a ¼" space between them. This forms the hinge.

The book's pages will be formed from sheets of 8½" × 11" unruled
paper folded along the width. This will give you four sides to a sheet, each
5½" × 8½" (the same as the literary magazine). In other words, six folded
sheets will yield twenty-four pages. Let's say that you have about twenty
pages of material. After folding the six pages together, number each page
lightly in pencil so that you'll know which page comes next. (You can erase
the numbers later.) Then separate the pages so that you can do the actual
printing job. I'd suggest leaving the first two pages blank, using the third for
the title and author, and the fourth for the copyright notice and/or dedica-
tion. The actual text will start on page five.

The next step is binding the pages together. You'll need a sheet of construction paper 9" × 12". Fold it in half across the width. Open the
assembled pages so that they lie flat, face up, on top of the construction paper, as shown. Sew the book pages to the construction paper down the fold.
You can do this by hand, using heavy-duty thread and a running stitch; or a
sewing machine may be used. In either case, double the stitching.

The construction paper is then glued to the inside of the covers. Finally, use another 9" strip of Mystik tape to form the outside spine of your book.

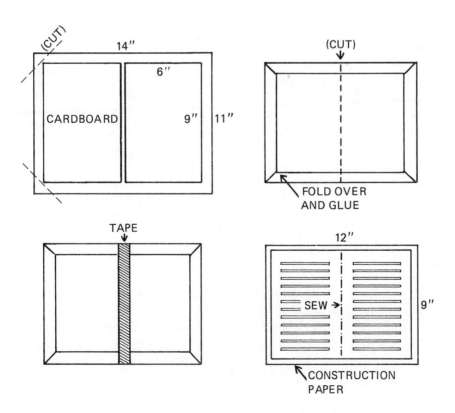

Appendix

Going Professional

Teachers who encourage students to use writing in the ways this book talks about don't see themselves as coaches preparing a handful of talented writers to make it to the pro ranks. Rather, they're concerned with helping every student become a competent writer—to find the writer that lives inside each of us, all of us. Writing well and eagerly is not the same as writing professionally. Few students (or adults, for that matter) will become professional writers, even minor leaguers. Forget the glamorous stories you've heard about writing for a living—about authors who make millions, sell their novels to Hollywood, and turn up on talk shows. For every celebrity writer there are thousands more you'll never hear of—men and women who work either part- or fulltime as writers for low pay and long hours. Supermarket clerks earn more on the average than all but a small percentage of people who are paid for their words.

Still, it's fun to get published, and some students can be, often those who sense only vaguely that they'd like to try, maybe just once, but don't know how to go about it. Sooner or later you may produce a piece of writing that you and others think is good enough to be shared by a wider, different audience than those in school and at home. Perhaps you already have such a piece, or many of them. The article below should be exciting to you. Its author deals firsthand with her own experiences as a writer. Not only does she explain how she gets her writing published; she also speaks simply and honestly about what the problems are.

Chronicle

Amy Dockser

By day I am a mild-mannered tenth grader, but by night, after all my homework is done, I become a writer.

My writing career began six years ago after I received a letter from my pen pal in Israel. Her letter had brought back memories of my trip there two summers before. I decided to write a poem and enclose it in my next letter to her.

Later that night, I thought about the poem. The words and ideas had flowed easily, but most important of all, my parents had loved it! Weeks later, I returned home to find an official-looking envelope awaiting me. When I looked at the letter, I realized that it was stamped with the seal of the Israeli government. It was from the mayor of Jerusalem. My pen pal, an employee of the mayor, had shown him the poem. He complimented me on what he felt was an accurate portrait of Jerusalem. I was nine years old then, and imagine my surprise that such an important man would take time out from his busy schedule to write to me!

This first success encouraged me to continue writing. However, writing was merely a hobby, something that was fun and was to be saved for when I had spare time.

This all changed when I received a letter from *Stone Soup,* a magazine that is written by and for children, about an article I had submitted. "We like your book review," the letter read. "We'd like to publish it." I received no pay, but I didn't care. Someone was actually reading my writing! After appearing in four more issues, I decided to write a letter to the editor of our weekly town newspaper, *The Lexington Minuteman.* That was my first query letter, and in it I asked to join their staff. After a personal interview with the editor, I was hired as their weekly children's book reviewer—and I was only 12 at the time. At first I was paid $5 per review, but since then my salary has been raised to $7.

It was there that my writing started to develop. I began reading books about writers, and this constant reading inspired me.

At first, I submitted articles to magazines they couldn't possibly fit in. My writing was unpolished, yet I submitted to top national magazines like *McCall's, Redbook, Ms.* and *The New Yorker.* I sooned learned about simple writing rules, however, and I began submitting articles to magazines that were within my reach. It was then that the problems of being a teenager *and* a writer began.

First of all, I cannot work all day perfecting a piece of writing. Homework and extracurricular events keep me very busy, and I must squeeze my writing into my schedule. My biggest problem, though, is my lack of mobility. If I want to attend an event that is farther away than my bicycling capabilities can take me, one of my parents must drive me. One time I had to be driven to Boston University because I was working on a column for a student newspaper whose office was located there. When my mother drove up to the school, picketing teachers greeted us with signs and angry expressions! My mother was supposed to drop me off and return later on, and I was afraid to enter the building alone. I kept envisioning an angry teacher grabbing me and yelling at me because I was crashing the picket line! Luckily, nobody paid attention to my entrance into the building.

Also, if I call a person for information and she must return the call the next day, I am in school and cannot receive the call. As a result, my mother must take the message, and usually I forget to tell her I am expecting a call. It is then that I am greeted at the door by an astonished, "*Who* have you been calling now?" This was the case when I called the Boston police station with a question about archaic blue laws. My mother has still not recovered from the shock she felt when she picked up the phone and a police officer was asking to speak to me!

Sometimes people don't take me seriously. One time during an interview over the phone, my subject asked me my age. When I told him I was 14, I had to spend an extra ten minutes also telling him why anyone my age would be writing magazine articles! Another time I was asked whether I was in college. When I said no, the man asked me whether I was in high school. I whispered very softly, "Junior high."

I have been very lucky, however. My parents and teachers take me seriously, and even some of my friends have finally begun to come around! When I talk to a friend about writing, I expect one of three reactions: surprise, interest or laughter. Many are surprised that even though I write, I still enjoy the same things they do. Often this surprise leads to an interest in how and why I write, and whether or not I have had any success. Usually there is a lot of laughter, however, and they often tease me about my column in the town newspaper. My friends often call me "The Young Reader," which is my column's name. This can sometimes become embarrassing, as it was one time in a store when a lady bumped into me. "Hey," cried my friend, "that's the Young Reader you're knocking into!" Many times I have come into class late, only to be greeted by, "Here comes the Young Reader!", and the caption in my 1980 school yearbook reads, "Y.R."

However, when I am writing for publication, the one reaction I do not want to receive is laughter. So in a query letter, I never mention my age unless it directly affects the article, although I'm sure that I have given my secret away unintentionally many times!

For instance, the first time I received a go-ahead from an editor, I was delirious with joy. It was from the *Tri-State Trader*, and its editor, Kevin Tanzillo, proved to be an extremely patient man. As soon as I began the research I realized that I had a lot of questions. Mr. Tanzillo had written that if I had any questions I should write to him, and so I did. Five times. I often asked him questions about pictures or the magazine's requirements. After a few letters, I began to fear that I would chase away my first buyer by asking so many questions, so in my next letter I asked him if he minded me asking so many! His letter back to me began: "Don't feel that you are bothering me with your questions. I am glad to help." Thanks to him, writing my first article was not as difficult as I thought it would be, and I eventually received a check for $10, which I photocopied.

Since then, I have made one additional sale, which was to *The Lion* for $75. Every year in Lexington, there is an April 19th parade, and my article was about the ways the Lexington Lions participated in the parade.

This lack of sales is probably caused by another one of my problems as a teenaged writer. In many ways my writing still reads like a child wrote it. I compose articles using transitional phrases that appear in the essays I hand in for English class. I struggle to make my sentences flow but still have impact on all who read them, and I possess a childish jealousy, as well as awe, for writers who succeed where I fail. It discourages me when I read something that seems perfect—how I wish I had wrote it! But I am never content with this shortcoming, and, in fact, sometimes I am the extreme opposite. I will cut out entire paragraphs ruthlessly and then revise and retype.

The biggest difference between an adult and a teenaged writer, however, is that teenaged writers are different from everyone else! This fact was brought home to me when a feature about my writing career appeared in a local paper. At school the next day I found myself in the spotlight—it was not all positive, however. I endured many negative comments that hurt my feelings. For instance, the newspaper reporter had written, "Amy doesn't have much time to watch television, which many blame for the apparent lack of literacy among many of her peers." Some of the kids read the article quickly, and thought that it was *me* who was saying my peers were illiterate. Indignant, a few of the kids criticized me for being so snobby. Although I tried to explain that I hadn't said anything like that, many of them refused to accept my explanations.

Despite all these obstacles, however, I would never give up writing. Writing keeps my life in balance. Whenever I am mad, I tend to become overexcited. When I write it down, however, I can put everything in perspective. For instance, after the feature about me appeared, I was extremely upset and didn't know what to do. I felt all alone. I wrote down why I was upset, and then decided what to do. "I don't have to be everyone's friend, and please everyone. Be pleasant, take it all in stride. Remember who's who, where and what I am and what I want to be. A somebody. And every somebody has downs, too." After writing a few more pages I felt much better. The next day everything was back to normal. So by writing things down, I'm able to deal with or solve my problems.

This is what I like about writing the most. I know that whether I get a bad grade on a test or have a fight with a friend, there is one thing I can depend on. And that is my writing. A paper and pen will always be ready to listen to me.

Above all, writing gives my life a new and exciting dimension. I am able to experience a world many teenagers will never see, and, as a teenager, I am able to understand and experience firsthand a part of living that many adult writers cannot.

This is not a "how-to" article. It wasn't meant to be a blueprint for other young writers to follow. Amy Dockser talks only about her own experiences in getting published. What happens to you, should you choose to seek a wider audience for your writing, will be another story, although maybe just as interesting. Yet this article does reveal four factors that play a part in most writers' success in breaking into print: (1) a love of writing; (2) hard work; (3) luck; and (4) learning enough about available markets to find out where to send what.

There's no sense in discussing luck; either it's with you or against you. And you've already begun to realize, I hope, that good writing involves both love and labor. What you may not know, though, is how and where to find an outlet for your stuff. These suggestions and observations should help:

- Local and area newspapers are often delighted to print young writers. Almost all have a letters-to-the-editor section, and your opinions on issues and events will be treated with the same respect an adult's letter would receive. Furthermore, newspapers are often on the look-out for student reporters to cover sports events or other happenings of interest at school. Papers that serve rural districts usually rely on freelance reporters to write up weekly news concerning outlying communities. No reason why a young reporter can't serve in this role. Let your paper know that you want to write. Have some specific suggestions in mind. It's not unusual for smaller papers to use young writers to review books and movies; write a hobbyists' column; or even an advice to teenagers feature. Human interest stories appear regularly in most papers. Do you know someone others would be interested in reading about—a person with an interesting job, hobby, lifestyle? Probably.
- No matter how small your school is, the English department receives announcements about writing contests of all kinds. Ask your teacher to please post and call to your attention any and all invitations to compete. Awards are often cash prizes, sometimes even scholarships.
- Many school districts, regional presses, literary groups, and other public and private sources sponsor literary magazines that publish only school-age writers. Your chances for publication in this kind of magazine are, I've found, quite good. Your library and English department should have copies of such publications. Study them before submitting your material. (This rule holds for *any* publication you're thinking about approaching. Editors reject stuff just as often because it doesn't fit as because the writing's poor. It's a waste of time submitting an essay to a magazine that publishes only short fiction; or a piece of short fiction to a publication that specializes in poetry.)
- There are hundreds of so-called "little magazines" that publish unknown, first-time writers. Some of these magazines have been in business for many years; others come and go overnight. Most of them specialize in poetry and short fiction. A "little magazine" is just that — small in size and circulation. But the thrill connected with having something of yours published in one of these magazines won't be small at all. Not that getting published in one of these sources is easy. Regardless of size, all magazines look for good material that will interest readers. The advantages of submitting your work to little magazines

are that they generally like to encourage new writers and that there are so many of them to choose from. At least one of those hundreds of editors may like what you've written.

- You may be surprised to learn that a number of national publications feature school-age writers, either in special sections or overall. While these magazines get flooded with material, keep in mind that none of it is from professionals. Your chances are as good as any other young writer's, especially if you bother to study back issues to find out what kinds of writing these publications are likely to be attracted by.
- Although getting published in a major commercial magazine—the kind carried on newsstands, with tons of ads and color sections— seems an impossible dream, few if any such publications refuse to publish pieces by young, unknown writers. For them the question is the same as it is for the smallest of little magazines: Is the piece good, and is it right for our audience? Submit your work to a major magazine (*Seventeen*, for example), and you're going up against good writers and lots of them. But don't forget luck, along with your own talent. And re-member too that it costs no more to mail your material to one of these magazines than it does to send it to the *Frostpond Gazette*.

*   *   *

Following are a few observations about how to prepare and send your writing; then a short list of writers' directories.

- Any material you submit should be typed. If it's prose—an article or short story—have it typed double space. Poetry is usually single space. It's okay to submit just one poem, but a standard procedure is to submit four or five at a time. Whatever you send, make an original, not a machine or carbon copy. Be sure your name appears on every page you submit, and include page numbers on works of more than one page. Don't staple pages together; editors prefer paperclips. It's stand-ard procedure to include a cover letter too, stating that you're submit-ting the enclosed material for possible publication and that it hasn't been published elsewhere. (If it has, say where.) Whenever possible, send your material to a specific someone, not just "Editor." (Who? I'll get to that.)
- Don't spend time telling your reader how good your stuff is or why it's right for the publication. That won't persuade anyone. If you think that a little background information, either about you or the material, will be useful, include it. Otherwise, let your writing speak for itself. Should you include your age? A *Seventeen* editor, Catherine Winters, says, "I personally like to see [a writer's] age. I think it makes the man-uscript more interesting. Of course, anything that is well-written is well-written. However, a piece that is written by a 19-year-old may not

be as impressive as it would be if it were written by a 14-year-old."

- Unless you include a stamped, self-addressed envelope, you won't get your stuff back. Make sure to keep a copy of your material anyhow. The one time you don't will be the time an editor misplaces a treasured poem or short story and it will be gone forever. How long will it take to find out whether your work has been accepted or rejected? It varies, but figure on at least a month, unless you're dealing with a local paper. That's a long time to keep your fingers crossed, but bear in mind that editors get heaps of material and to do a fair job of judging takes time. Also, some editors take the trouble to write a personal letter rather than just sending a rejection notice. I've known writers young and old who were delighted with the encouraging words an editor sent along with a rejection.

- Your school or local library may carry a directory of markets for writers. In it will be listed names and addresses of magazines and other markets, along with such details as an editor's name, types of materials the publication seeks, minimum and maximum lengths of pieces, information about how they prefer material to be submitted, approximate time between receiving and responding to materials, readership, circulation, and terms of payment (if any). You can submit material, perhaps successfully, without consulting such a directory, but the information they contain is extremely useful in helping a writer find and approach the right places. If you can't locate a copy of the following directories in your library, ask that they be ordered:
Writer's Market, 9933 Alliance Road, Cincinnati, OH 45242.
Fiction Writer's Market (same address as above).
The International Directory of Little Magazines and Small Presses, P.O. Box 100, Paradise, CA 95969.

These periodicals are useful too, not just for the markets they list but also for their articles on writing for publication:

Coda, Poets & Writers, Inc., 201 West 54th Street, New York, NY 10019.
The Writer, 8 Arlington Street, Boston, MA 02116.
Writer's Digest, 9933 Alliance Road, Cincinnati, OH 45242.
Writer's Yearbook (same address as above).

To find out more about these magazines, write for a sample copy.

*   *   *

The aim of this book is to encourage you to discover what writing can mean to you and nobody else. It isn't to convince you that getting published is the final, or even the important, goal. Sending an important part of yourself to a stranger for judgment is kind of scary. Ask anyone who's done it. And unless you're extremely lucky, the judgment will be against you, regardless of how good that piece of you may be. Maybe that's not for you. If you're quick to lose confidence in yourself, or not yet ready to put your writing to a public test, don't let yourself be argued into it. If readers you trust think something you've done is worth publishing—and if you agree—give it a try, and then another try, and then a few more tries after that.

If you can't stand rejection, Herbert,
stop sending out that same godawful poem!

Answers to riddles on pp. 51 and 52:

1. See you in September.
2. This is a picture of an early bird that caught a very strong worm.
3. Leave well enough alone.
4. You can't teach an old dog new tricks.
5. His grandma falling ott.

Constellations:

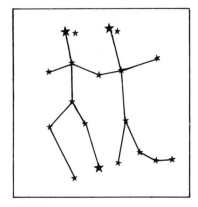

Gemini

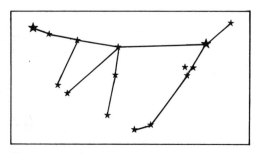

Capricorn